The Globalization of Christianity

McMaster Divinity College Press
Theological Studies Series 6  McMaster Divinity College

Defining Issues in Pentecostalism (2008)

Pentecostalism and Globalization (2009)

You Mean I Don't Have to Tithe? (2009)

Baptism (2011)

Resurrection, Scripture, and Reformed Apologetics (2012)

The Globalization of Christianity
Implications for Christian Ministry and Theology

edited by
GORDON L. HEATH
and
STEVEN M. STUDEBAKER

☙PICKWICK *Publications* · Eugene, Oregon

THE GLOBALIZATION OF CHRISTIANITY
Implications for Christian Ministry and Theology

McMaster Divinity College Theological Studies Series 6

Copyright © 2014 Wipf and Stock Publishers. All rights reserved. Except for brief quotations in critical publications or reviews, no part of this book may be reproduced in any manner without prior written permission from the publisher. Write: Permissions. Wipf and Stock Publishers, 199 W. 8th Ave., Suite 3, Eugene, OR 97401.

McMaster Divinity College Press
1280 Main Street West
Hamilton, Ontario, Canada
L8S 4K1

Pickwick Publications
An Imprint of Wipf and Stock Publishers
199 W. 8th Ave., Suite 3
Eugene, OR 97401

www.wipfandstock.com

ISBN 13: 978-1-62564-801-3

Cataloguing-in-Publication Data

> The Globalization of Christianity: Implications for Christian Ministry and Theology / edited by Gordon L. Heath and Steven M. Studebaker
>
> xiv + 166 p. ; 23 cm. Includes bibliographical references.
>
> ISBN 13: 978-1-62564-801-3
>
> 1. Globalization—Religious aspects—Christianity. 2. Church and the World. I. Title.

BR115 W6 G5 2014

Manufactured in the U.S.A.   12/08/2014

Scripture marked NRSV is taken from the New Revised Standard Version Bible, copyright 1989, Division of Christian Education of the National Council of the Churches of Christ in the United States of America. Used by permission. All rights reserved.

Scripture marked TNIV is taken from the Holy Bible, Today's New International Version.™ Copyright © 2001 by International Bible Society. All rights reserved.

Table of Contents

Abbreviations / vii

About the Contributors / ix

1 Introduction: Globalization, Christendom, Theology, Ministry, and Mission—*Steven M. Studebaker* and *Bradley K. Broadhead* / 1

2 Changes and Trends in Global Christianity—*Philip Jenkins* / 15

3 New Models of Ministry in Canada as a Response to the Decline of Western Christianity—*Lee Beach* / 31

4 Servants of Christ, Servants of Caesar: A Theology for Life in Post-Christian America—*Steven M. Studebaker* / 52

5 Cross-Cultural Preaching: Proclaiming a Global Faith —*Michael P. Knowles* / 69

6 Soaking Prayer and the Advancement of the Kingdom of Love: Charismatic Renewal as Mission—*Peter Althouse* and *Michael Wilkinson* / 85

7 "Thor and Allah . . . in a hideous, unholy confederacy": The Armenian Genocide in the Canadian Protestant Press—*Gordon L. Heath* / 105

Table of Contents

   8 A Theology of Persecution and Martyrdom: An Example in Globalizing Theology—*Christof Sauer* / 129

   9 Global Christianity: Eyewitness Reflections from Iraq, Kenya, and South Korea—*John Haitham Issak, David Kirwa Tarus, Seongho Kang* / 140

      Author Index / 159

      Subject Index / 163

      Scripture Index / 165

Abbreviations

KJV King James (Authorized) Version

NPNF *Nicene and Post-Nicene Fathers*, First Series. Edited by Alexander Robertson, James Donaldson, Philip Schaff, and Henry Wase. 2nd ed. Peabody, MA: Hendrickson, 1996.

NRSV New Revised Standard Version

TDNT *Theological Dictionary of the New Testament.* 10 vols. Edited by Gerhard Kittell and Gerhard Friedrich. Translated by Geoffrey W. Bromiley. Grand Rapids: Eerdmans, 1964–76.

TNIV Today's New International Version

About the Contributors

EDITORS AND CONTRIBUTORS

Gordon L. Heath (PhD, St. Michael's College) is Associate Professor of Christian History at McMaster Divinity College, and serves as Director of the Canadian Baptist Archives. His recent appointment to the Centenary Chair in World Christianity at the college reflects his growing interest in the elimination of Christian communities around the world. His publications include *A War with a Silver Lining: Canadian Protestant Churches and the South African War, 1899–1902* (2009), and *Doing Church History: A User-friendly Introduction to Researching the History of Christianity* (2008). He has a forthcoming book on British, Australian, Canadian, New Zealand, and South African Baptist attitudes to late nineteenth-century imperialism (Paternoster). He has also recently edited *Canadian Churches and the First World War* (2014), and co-edited *Canadian Baptists and Public Life* (2012), and *Baptism: Historical, Theological, and Pastoral Perspectives* (2011).

Steven M. Studebaker (PhD, Marquette University) is Associate Professor of Systematic and Historical Theology, and Howard and Shirley Bentall Chair in Evangelical Thought at McMaster Divinity College. He teaches courses on theology and culture, as well as traditional theological topics. He is the author of three books on Jonathan Edwards's trinitarian theology (*Jonathan Edwards' Social Augustinian Trinitarianism in Historical and Contemporary Perspectives*, *The Trinitarian Theology of Jonathan Edwards and David Coffey*, and *The Trinitarian Theology of Jonathan Edwards: Text, Context, and Application*); several edited books on the way globalization transforms the context of contemporary Christian

About the Contributors

thought, life, and ministry (*Pentecostalism and Globalization*, *Defining Issues in Pentecostalism* and *The Liberating Spirit*); and the recent book *From Pentecost to the Triune God*.

CONTRIBUTORS

Peter Althouse (PhD, St. Michael's College) is Professor of Religion and Theology at Southeastern University, Florida. Publications include (with Michael Wilkinson) *Catch the Fire: Soaking Prayer and Charismatic Renewal* (Northern Illinois University Press); *Spirit of the Last Days: Pentecostal Eschatology in Conversation with Jürgen Moltmann* (T. & T. Clark); *The Ideological Development of Power in Early American Pentecostalism* (Edwin Mellen Press); (with Michael Wilkinson) *Winds from the North: Canadian Contributions to the Pentecostal Movement* (Brill); and (with Robby Waddell) *Perspectives in Pentecostal Eschatologies* (Pickwick).

Lee Beach (PhD, McMaster Divinity College) is Assistant Professor of Christian Ministry, Director of Ministry Formation, and Garbutt F. Smith Chair of Ministry Formation at McMaster Divinity College in Hamilton, Ontario, where he teaches courses on pastoral ministry, the church in culture, and Christian spirituality. Lee pastored for eighteen years with the Christian and Missionary Alliance in Canada and is currently involved in a church plant in Ancaster, Ontario. He is the author of *The Church in Exile: Living in Hope after Christendom* (IVP).

Bradley K. Broadhead (MA, Ambrose University College) is a doctoral candidate in Christian Theology at McMaster Divinity College, Hamilton, Ontario. His research interests lie in the intersection between music and theology. He is writing his dissertation on how jazz improvisation can be used analogically to expand and contextualize a biblical understanding of Christian freedom in a postmodern context. His interest in globalization is linked to his interest in post-Christendom and postmodernism.

John Haitham Issak was born in Nineveh, Iraq. He finished four years of studies in Syriac Orthodox Seminary of Mosul in Nineveh. He was award-

About the Contributors

ed a BA in theology at the University of Athens, Greece. In 1999–2000, he served as a director of the Syriac Seminary in Mosul. In 2000–2001, he lectured in Patrology and Greek language at the Syriac Orthodox Seminary of Damascus (Syria), and in 2001, emigrated to Canada to serve as pastor to the Syriac Orthodox Church in Hamilton. He earned an MTS (2006) and a Diploma in Eastern Christian Studies (2008) at St. Michael's College, University of Toronto. He is currently a pastor of two Syriac Orthodox Churches in Hamilton and Burlington, as well as a PhD student in Christian Theology at McMaster Divinity College.

Philip Jenkins was educated at Cambridge University. From 1980 through 2011 he taught at Penn State University, where he holds the rank of Emeritus Edwin Erle Sparks Professor of Humanities. In 2012 he became a Distinguished Professor of History at Baylor University, where he also serves in the Institute for Studies of Religion. He has published 25 books, including *The Next Christendom: The Coming of Global Christianity* (2002), *The Lost History of Christianity* (2008), and *The Great and Holy War* (2014).

Seongho Kang is an ordained pastor of the Korean Presbyterian Church (Kosin), as well as a PhD student in Christian Ethics at McMaster Divinity College. He graduated from Seoul National University (BEng), Korea Theological Seminary (MDiv), and Calvin Theological Seminary (ThM). He served as a researcher for the Christian Ethics Movement of Korea for one year, where he edited a book entitled *Christian Response toward Homosexuality*. As a representative of the Institute, he participated in panel discussions for controversial issues in Christian ethics. He also drafted several statements concerning Christian ethics in the area of church and society. Since working with the Christian Ethics Movement of Korea, which conducted surveys on social credibility for South Korean churches, he has been very interested in helping Korean churches to recover social credibility in the public square.

Michael P. Knowles took his undergraduate studies in Victoria and Quebec City, and completed an MDiv (1982) and a ThD in New Testament (1991) at Wycliffe College, Toronto. Ordained within the Anglican Church of Canada, he has since 1997 held the George Franklin Hurlburt Chair of Preaching at McMaster Divinity College in Hamilton,

Ontario. In addition to articles in the fields of Old Testament, New Testament, intertestamental studies, pastoral theology, homiletics, and evangelism, and an edited volume of lectures and sermons (*The Folly of Preaching: Models and Methods*, Eerdmans, 2007), his publications include *Jeremiah in Matthew's Gospel: The Rejected-Prophet Motif in Matthaean Redaction* (JSOT, 1993), *We Preach Not Ourselves: Paul on Preaching* (Brazos, 2008), and *The Unfolding Mystery of the Divine Name: The God of Sinai in Our Midst* (IVP, 2012). His most recent study (forthcoming from Wipf & Stock/Cascade) engages New Testament theology and the spirituality of preaching, and is provisionally titled *Of Seeds and the People of God: Preaching as Parable, Crucifixion, and Testimony*. His research and teaching interests include homiletics, worship, and biblical interpretation, focusing in particular on the theological foundations of the church's mission and ministry.

Christof Sauer is Professor of Religious Studies and Missiology at the Evangelical Theological Faculty in Leuven, Belgium. His special research focus is religious freedom and persecution. He is also Co-Director of the International Institute for Religious Freedom (Bonn–Cape Town–Colombo) of the World Evangelical Alliance and is based in Cape Town, South Africa. In 2013, he was appointed visiting lecturer (Privatdozent) at the Protestant University in Wuppertal, Germany. At this institution he completed a postdoctoral degree (Habilitation) with a thesis on martyrdom and mission, comparing selected positions in global Christianity, sponsored in part by Voice of the Martyrs Canada. He is also Associate Professor Extraordinary at the Department of Practical Theology and Missiology, Stellenbosch University, South Africa, and an external supervisor of doctoral students at the Department of Christian Spirituality, Church History and Missiology, University of South Africa, where he received his doctorate in missiology in 2002. He edited *Suffering, Persecution and Martyrdom–Evangelical Theological Reflections*, and is founding editor of the *International Journal for Religious Freedom*. Sauer is an ordained pastor of his home church province, the Evangelical Lutheran Church in Württemberg, Germany.

David Kirwa Tarus is a native of Kenya and a PhD student in Christian Theology at McMaster Divinity College in Hamilton, Ontario, Canada. He is a graduate of Scott Theological College, Kenya (BTh), and

About the Contributors

Wheaton College Graduate School (MA Theology). He has previously worked as the coordinator of Scott Theological College, Eldoret Campus, in Kenya. He is a beneficiary of Billy Graham, Langham Partnership, and ScholarLeaders International scholarships. His published works include "Social Transformation in the Circle of Concerned African Women Theologians," and "The Significance of Intellectual Humility for Theologians Today," in the *Africa Journal of Evangelical Theology*. His research interests are in the areas of theological anthropology, ethnicity, and ecclesiology.

Michael Wilkinson (PhD, University of Ottawa) is Professor of Sociology, Director of the Religion in Canada Institute, and coordinator of the Canadian Pentecostal Research Network, Trinity Western University. Publications include: *The Spirit Said Go: Pentecostal Immigrants in Canada*; *Canadian Pentecostalism: Transition and Transformation*; *Winds from the North: Canadian Contributions to the Pentecostal Movement* (with Peter Althouse); and *A Liberating Spirit: Pentecostals and Social Action in North America* (with Steven Studebaker). He is also co-editor with Peter Althouse of the *Canadian Journal of Pentecostal-Charismatic Christianity*.

1

Introduction
Globalization, Christendom,
Theology, Ministry, and Mission

Steven M. Studebaker and Bradley K. Broadhead

From a Western perspective, Christianity is in a state of decline. In nations that once strongly identified with the Christian faith, it has lost its cultural dominance. Fewer and fewer people attend church, and increasingly, people adhere to no religion whatsoever. The signs are indeed disturbing for some and a cause for celebration for others (ironically among non-Christians and Christians alike), but they paint an incomplete picture. Philip Jenkins has done much to disabuse us of the common perception that Christianity is a Western religion, vigorously defending the fact that, on the contrary, "Christianity has never been synonymous with either Europe or the West."[1] And when the world as a whole is taken into consideration, one inevitably comes to the conclusion "that since 1700 Christianity has undergone its greatest period of expansion ever, and is currently more vigorous, healthy and widely embraced than at any previous time."[2] This growth is occurring in the Global South, in areas often characterized by poverty and conflict. The nature of globalization complicates matters by bringing the world closer together through immigration and advances in information technology. Christianity in its southern form is moving north as nations

1. Jenkins, *Next Christendom*, 24.
2. Hylson-Smith, *Ends of the Earth*, xxv.

facing population stagnation find that they must welcome others in order to sustain themselves economically and socially. It also finds itself bumping up against Islam, a formidable competitor. All of these factors have an impact on the way Western Christians do theology and ministry, which is what this book is about.

A Brief Outline of the Rise and Fall of Christendom

Any discussion of contemporary Christianity and globalization is incomplete without reference to the story of Christendom. The history of globalization can be divided into (1) the fifteenth-century Iberian discoveries of much of the rest of the world, (2) the mercantilism of the eighteenth century, (3) the European imperialism of the nineteenth century, and (4) the postcolonial aftermath of the Second World War.[3] The first three of these stages are closely tied to Christendom. The colonial actions of European powers accelerated the process of globalization and shaped the political, social, and religious circumstances of the rest of the world. These actions were intimately linked to the values and ambitions of Christendom. Understanding the origins of Christendom will aid in understanding both its legacy and its decline. This historical perspective on Christendom in turn will underline the significance of the Christianities emerging in the Global South and the importance of heeding their voices in the West.

Though Christendom emerged in the Roman Empire (Western and Byzantine) and later among the Franks, it reigned as the dominant model of Christianity in the West from the eleventh to the early part of the twentieth century. Leaving behind its status as a minority religion, Christianity became synonymous with Western society: "the church was the entire society and the entire society was the church."[4] The origins of this state of affairs trace back to the conversion of the Germanic peoples.[5] Germanic identity was strongly rooted in the idea of a common custom held by all.

---

3. See Kalu, "Globalization and Mission," 25.
4. Hanciles, *Beyond Christendom*, 84.
5. Some trace it back to Constantine (e.g., Murray, *Post-Christendom*, 24–38). But Andrew Walls makes a convincing case that "The Roman Empire is not the place to seek the birth of Christendom," arguing that instead the "cement" that held Christendom together for so long is found in the nature of the conversion of the Germanic peoples (see below) (Walls, "Ecumenical Missiology," 192).

Introduction

Since religion was an element essential to custom, it was out of the question for members of the society to ascribe to different belief systems. Instead of being something to be privately accepted or rejected by the individual, Christianity was to be publicly accepted or rejected by all. While the model of individual conversion still held true in some cases, more often a ruler or chieftain would convert and then his subjects or tribe would follow en masse.[6] Missionaries and rulers found working together mutually beneficial; the former found an efficient way of converting whole tribes and kingdoms (and enjoyed royal protection, generous endowments, and a lift in status) while the latter "acquired new grandeur and renown, were introduced to new techniques of rule in literacy and legislation, [and] benefited from notions or rituals which enhanced the authority and mystique of royalty."[7] Though at times these conversions were (allegedly) voluntary,[8] at other times Christian rulers seeking to add more territory to their domain forced conquered peoples to convert.[9] Though it was a long struggle, Christendom gained such ascendency over Europe "that European culture was seen as Christian culture."[10]

Given the strong connection between Christendom and custom, law, society, and politics, it is not surprising that it was rather intolerant of any sort of religious dissent. While Jewish and Muslim minorities were generally (but not always) tolerated, they were deliberately marginalized and given few rights. Groups deemed heretical such as the Cathars were given the options of recanting or being exterminated. The Protestant Reformation movements assumed Christendom. The Anabaptists rejected it and were subject to persecution by Protestants and Catholics. The terrible Thirty Years War (1618–48), and its so-called Wars of Religion, did more, at least in the short run, to buttress than undermine Christendom.[11] The very terms of the Peace of Westphalia, under which the ruler determined the religion of their region, made it clear that the model of Christendom would be maintained by Catholics and Protestants alike.

6. Walls, "Ecumenical Missiology," 192–93.
7. Fletcher, *Barbarian Conversion*, 237.
8. See Bede, *Ecclesiastical History*, 1.26.
9. Take for example the conquests of Charlemagne.
10. Hanciles, *Beyond Christendom*, 90.
11. Cavanaugh critiques the widely held view that the Thirty Years War was the result of divisiveness and intolerance among Christians. It was the product of the emerging ideologies of nation states. See Cavanaugh, *Theopolitical Imagination*.

3

One result of making Christianity a state religion was that mission was synonymous with territorial expansion.[12] One simply did not take on a mission without the support and sanction of political authorities. According to Jehu Hanciles, "With no exception, European nations . . . believed that their territorial acquisitions were divinely ordained for the expansion of the gospel of salvation."[13] Territorial acquisition was seen as a sign of divine favor, which in turn spurred on greater missionary activity. A sense of calling by certain people groups appears to be linked to a strong understanding of the "gospel of Christ [as] a truly universal ethic that must be proclaimed to all nations."[14] Yet these national interests also hampered the effectiveness of missionaries by working against attempts at international collaboration, especially between Protestants. Missionary activity went hand in hand with conquest, economic exploitation, nationalist competition, and ethnocentrism. Highlighting this connection ought not to deface the accomplishments of principled, self-sacrificing missionaries who carried out their ministries in the far-flung lands of colonial empires with sincere devotion to Christ. It does, however, acknowledge the uneasy confluence of national and religious aims that was Christendom.

Other aspects of Christendom often also stifled mission. Portuguese Catholics, for instance, refused to ordain native clergy in Africa, crippling the church in the African Kingdom of Kongo. By insisting on the rule of European bishops, they left the church without the resources to propagate or even maintain itself. At times the very fabric of Christendom began to unravel; the connection between the aims of Christianity and the aims of commerce and empire were often at odds with one another. For example, Muslims under the British Empire could not be evangelized by eager British missionaries because colonial rule relied on Islamic infrastructures. Similarly, the East India Company initially prohibited missionaries from working in India for fear of upsetting a profitable status quo. Inconsistencies like these exposed the disparate goals of faith and empire.[15]

The Bible itself, however, delivered the death knell of missional Christendom. As it was translated into the languages of numerous peoples, its

---

12. Anabaptist groups that rejected the Christendom model were notable exceptions to this rule.

13. Hanciles, *Beyond Christendom*, 96.

14. Stanley, "Christianity," 5.

15. For more on the complex and conflicted relationship between missions and empire, see Porter, *Religion versus Empire?*

message inspired resistance to colonial control. Lamin Sanneh suggests that, "[b]y their root conviction that the gospel is transmissible in the mother tongue . . . missionaries opened the way for the local idiom to gain the ascendancy over assertions of foreign superiority."[16] Adrian Hastings has even argued that the notion of nationhood is linked to the Bible.[17] When colonies began to view themselves as nations in their own right, empires began to crumble. At this point, the goal of extending Western Christendom to the rest of the world, if it ever was tenable, had to be abandoned entirely. Although many churches and denominations with European origins remain in the non-Western world as a testimony to the great missionary activity of the West, a closer examination reveals that these are not clones but are strongly colored by local culture and custom, distancing the link between European Christendom and Christianity in the former areas of European empires.

The centuries-old relationship between society and faith that defined Christendom is giving way. Societal practice has become separate from faith. Hanciles argues that the "massive de-Christianization" of the West is linked in part to "a diminished sense of mission to its own society and culture."[18] This loss of missional vitality in turn arises from the old (con)fusion of Christianity with European culture. In 1943, William Temple, Archbishop of Canterbury, warned that the "Christian tradition . . . was in danger of being undermined by a 'Secular Humanism' which hoped to retain Christian values without Christian faith."[19] Secular humanism has since disavowed its Christian roots and seeks to establish a morality independent of God on philosophical and scientific grounds.[20] Yet the gains of atheism should not be exaggerated; many Europeans hold on to notions of Christian spirituality, however vague they may have become.[21] Whatever post-Christendom ultimately entails, it cannot easily erase the marks of Christianity on Europe. The vibrant forms of Christianity in the Global South similarly bear the marks of European Christendom, but this

16. Sanneh, *Encountering the West*, 19.
17. See Hastings, *Construction of Nationhood*, especially 185–209.
18. Hanciles, *Beyond Christendom*, 110.
19. "Free Church Ministers in Anglican Pulpits."
20. According to Stephen Law, "Even if, as a matter of historical fact, our modern liberal values were originally argued for on religious grounds, moral and political philosophers have developed a whole range of justifications on which we can also draw" (Law, *Humanism*, 106).
21. See Hylson-Smith, *Ends of the Earth*, 171–79.

Christianity is not a Western religion; it stands on its own and is more than capable of resisting Western trends that it perceives to be guided more by Western culture than Scripture. Hopefully, the experience of Christendom in the West will serve as an effective warning against making the same mistakes in the Global South.

The wane of Western Christendom by no means entailed a corresponding decline in Christianity. In fact, as Jenkins notes, "[i]t was precisely as Western colonialism ended that Christianity began a period of explosive growth that still continues unchecked."[22] In spite of the way that Christendom hampered their efforts, the seeds sown by Western missionaries bore fruit. In many places, they were not forging ahead into virgin territory but "reopening ancient and quite familiar mines" where Christianity had already made a mark.[23] This reopening was by no means insignificant; at best it revitalized a fading faith and at the very least it restored contact between Christians long separated by time and space. The work of Western missionaries was instrumental in beginning the process of constructing a global conception of the church, which, as we will show below, has much to contribute to theology, ministry, and mission. Indeed, scholars ought to be wary of engaging in "chronological snobbery" towards European missionary effort; the post-Christian West of the present age will likely be found wanting in several areas by future generations.[24]

Globalizing Theology

The decline of Christendom and the corresponding shift of the center of Christianity to the Global South will inevitably entail a corresponding shift in the focus and method of theology. During the period in which missionary activity overlapped with Christendom, it seemed evident to colonial Christians that their theology was "a systematic set of universal truths" that only needed to be translated into other languages.[25] If truth was universal

22. Jenkins, *Next Christendom*, 70.

23. Ibid., 45.

24. C. S. Lewis coined the term "chronological snobbery" in *Surprised by Joy* (and credits the insight to Owen Barfield); it means "the uncritical acceptance of the intellectual climate common to our age and the assumption that whatever has gone out of date is on that account discredited" (Lewis, *Surprised by Joy*, 207). Certainly good reasons exist to be critical of the missionary work of the nineteenth century, but the contemporary tendency to throw the baby out with the bath water, so to speak, is short-sighted at best.

25. Netland, "Introduction," 28.

Introduction

and if their theology put truth forth systematically, it followed that their theology ought to be similarly universal. But after the Second World War, colonialism collapsed and, along with it, a Western sense of superiority.

Postcolonial thought impacted certain missiologists to the point where the pendulum swung the other way and "contextualization often became an uncritical process in which the good in other cultures was affirmed, but the evil in them was left unchallenged."[26] Theology was shorn of any previous ability to transcend a given locale. Some middle way that acknowledges the unifying principles of Christian theology while being versatile enough to engage with local concerns is perhaps the best way forward.[27] But these unifying principles must no longer be synonymous with Western theological formulations; they must be worked out with the global church. The failure of Christendom serves as a stark reminder that Western theology is not a pure distilment of universal truths. Theology must become global. Harold Netland is correct that "[g]lobalizing theology is theological reflection rooted in God's self-revelation in Scripture" and the historical and global voices of the Christian faith.[28]

The present challenge is how to engage with these "diverse perspectives." Tite Tiénou vents some of his frustrations with continued Western scholarly hegemony in his essay, "Christian Theology in an Era of World Christianity." After pointing out that most Christians live in the Global South,[29] he bemoans the incongruous dominance of Western theology. Theological scholarship from the Global South is often treated as an exotic addition to mainstream Western scholarship. Tiénou continues, the "'standard' textbooks of systematic theology either lack any reference to theologians of non-European descent or contain only passing references to some without significant interaction with their ideas."[30] If globalizing theology is to become a reality, this state of affairs cannot persist; Western scholars must make a point of addressing the critiques and concerns of the rest of the Christian world.

Engaging with theology from diverse sources can correct the myopia that can occur from drawing one's theological sources from a singular cultural context. Theology can and must speak to a local context, but it must

26. Hiebert, *Anthropological Reflections*, 59.
27. For a proposal along these lines, see Hiebert, "Metatheology."
28. Netland, "Introduction," 30.
29. See Jenkins's chapter below for an assessment of this phenomenon.
30. Tiénou, "Christian Theology," 50.

also engage with the concerns of the world-wide church and be willing to engage in mutually edifying and corrective dialogue over these concerns. As Kevin J. Vanhoozer argues, "[l]ocation should never become the essential characteristic of theology."[31] For Vanhoozer, Scripture remains the primary source for theology and doctrines such as the Trinity remain essential traits of Christianity regardless of location. Neither Western presuppositions and methods nor local theologies are above being called to account. If Western theology can act as an antidote to syncretism in the Global South, so too can the theologians of Global South call into question Western theology influenced by the powerful forces of Western secular culture. Humility and open ears are both required to reap the benefits of the mutually corrective and edifying voices of global theology.

Mission and Ministry in an Era of World Christianity

An approach to mission and ministry in a Western context must confront the specter of post-Christendom. While, as Jenkins and others point out below, Christianity in the Global South is doing very well indeed, "Christians in post-Christendom are abnormal: our wealth, whiteness, declining numbers, experience of secularization and postmodernity, weariness and struggle to adjust to marginality are exceptional within the global church."[32] Stuart Murray examines several possible ways of responding to post-Christendom before settling on "disavowing" Christendom. This entails being open and honest about the dark side of its history and letting go of it as a system for gaining and maintaining political and social powers and privileges. This is not the same thing as repudiating the Christianity that held Europe for the past fifteen hundred years, but rather a celebration of the fact that the Christian faith is no longer compulsive. In terms of the rest of the world, hopefully Christianity can lose its stigma as a Western religion.

Whatever the positive aspects of post-Christendom, the decline of the Western churches is nothing to celebrate. Christians in the West are hurting in spite of their monetary assets (though these are also declining in independent churches). Those seeking to evangelize their neighbors have a challenging path ahead, caught between the evaporating influences of Christendom on the one hand and the assumption that Christianity is

---

31. Vanhoozer, "One Rule," 106.
32. Murray, *Post-Christendom*, 16.

a relic of establishment values on the other. Old techniques and methods of ministering and evangelizing based on the assumption of Christendom need to be reconsidered. New ways of doing church and mission need to be explored and evaluated. Any remnant of a feeling of superiority over the thriving churches in the South must be vanquished; the time has come for the West to learn from the example of others.[33]

Christians in the Global South are already responding to the crisis in the West. Missionaries from Africa are at work in the United Kingdom. Many Christians from the Global South are moving to the West in search of employment and security, bringing a vibrant faith born in their homelands to old churches.[34] Perhaps they can help to bring new life and vitality to old churches. The same forces of migration bring peoples who have not yet encountered the gospel into a Western context, opening up new opportunities and challenges for evangelism. Both situations call for heeding the biblical call to hospitality (e.g., Job 31:32; Matt 25:35; Rom 15:7; Heb 13:2). Christians in the West have the capacity to serve immigrant populations in many ways, from English as a Second Language (ESL) programs to financial aid and moral support.[35]

Finally, as missionaries from the Global South work to spread the gospel, they must be wary of repeating the mistakes of Christendom, namely of confusing national aspirations and motivations with a sense of God's calling. Missionaries in the West must let go of any lingering connection between patriotism and evangelizing. Moreover, if they are to be effective, they must not neglect the universal nature of the gospel. Perhaps in part out of guilt for past wrongs, liberal theology in the West during the twentieth century downplayed this universal nature. The challenge is "*not* to move from nationalism to universalism, but to find a way of abandoning nationalism *without also* weakening universalism."[36] The drive to evangelize is at the heart of the Christian faith, but it must be rooted in a biblical doctrine of ecclesiology and a desire for the glory of God if it is to avoid the mistakes of the past.

---

33. See Hylson-Smith, *Ends of the Earth*, 181.
34. See Pocock, Rheenen, and McConnell, *Changing Face*, 150–51.
35. For further discussion of hospitality and mission in the West, see ibid., 65–72.
36. Stanley, "Christianity," 6 (emphasis original).

Overview of This Book

The chapters of this book were first presented at a conference in 2011 on the globalization of Christianity, sponsored and hosted by the Theological Studies division of McMaster Divinity College in Hamilton, Ontario, Canada. Philip Jenkins was the plenary speaker, and gave three addresses. Shorter papers on a variety of subjects were also delivered. For a number of reasons not all of the shorter papers are published in this book. The only chapter in this book not a part of the original conference is the one by Issak, Tarus, and Kang.

Several key themes emerge in the following chapters when they are read in light of one another. First, the reality of persecution, especially in the Global South, demands attention in the form of theological, spiritual, and practical engagement. Second, the dynamics of globalization and post-Christendom require innovative ways of renewing ministry and mission in Western societies. Third, a strong link exists between supernaturalism and church growth in global Christianity.

Jenkins opens the body of this book with a magisterial survey of the issues faced by Christians around the world. He provides a bird's-eye view of trends in the growth of Christianity, highlighting the stability of Christianity's proportion of the world population, its growth in absolute terms, its growth in relation to Islam, and the parts of the world in which it is growing and where it is in decline. From this vantage point he identifies a number of trends in the Global South. In particular, growing churches in the Global South often share in common charismatic expressions of faith that embrace healing and spiritual warfare. Denominations and labels with a storied history in the West blur and combine in fresh ways. Moreover, in stark contrast to the majority status of Christianity long taken for granted in the West, Christianity in the Global South must compete with well-established rivals, especially Islam. Finally, these Christians offer ways of interpreting Scripture grounded in life experience that is closer in many ways to the world of the text.

Examining the nature of global Christianity raises several practical issues for the church. In his essay, Michael Knowles argues that the voices of the Global South ought not to be given special authority because they have been marginalized and hurt by the West (though they are by no means to be ignored); the locus of Christianity is the word of Scripture. He maintains that the Christian message is simultaneously culturally specific, supra-cultural, and counter-cultural. For Knowles, the crucifixion symbolizes the rejection of God's message by humanity, and its silence silences all other voices without exception. Instead of battling for "linguistic and cultural supremacy," he calls Christian preachers to testify to the things of God. Contrasting Babel with Pentecost, he argues that preachers ought not to presume to set the conditions of the divine-human encounter, but must entrust them instead to God. Preaching to different cultural groups entails both speaking to them in their own language and celebrating the transcendent acts of God that unify his people.

Christof Sauer provides a sober reminder of another practical issue for the global church: the reality of persecution and martyrdom. He reminds Christians in the West that fellow believers face these threats in a very real and immediate way. Scripture as a whole testifies to the fact that God allows his people to experience suffering. Christ provides the ultimate example. Sauer calls for solidarity with Christians who are suffering persecution, even across denominational lines. Martyrdom can lead to church growth, but it may also dissuade others from witnessing for Christ and even signal the silencing of a final voice in a given area.

Steven Studebaker focuses on the phenomenon emerging in the West known as post-Christendom. Although Christianity is a majority religion in parts of the Global South, it is becoming a minority in the West. Studebaker examines several attempts to wrestle with this emerging situation. Eschewing attempts to reassert Christendom in the West, he focuses instead on "Ghetto Christianity"—that is, approaches that aim to survive on the margins of society. The three main approaches he observes are (1) margins Christianity, which simultaneously rejects the project of Christendom and the dominant culture, (2) fortress Christianity, which attempts to defend a version of orthodoxy at all costs, and (3) club Christianity, which embraces a private faith and peace with the secular world. These approaches have in common a bifurcated view of life that Studebaker links to the theological split between common and special grace, between creation and redemption. His essay attempts to deconstruct this dichotomy by calling on Western Christians to be "citizen sojourners."

Lee Beech continues in the vein of post-Christendom, offering an analysis of trends in Canadian Christianity in the context of global Christianity. He sets the stage with statistics on declining church attendance in Canada and then examines how new movements are attempting to combat this trend by exploring different ways of doing church. These movements include formats such as house churches, internet church, and the new monastic communities (moving into a given area and living in a communal way). After considering the differences in various areas between these movements and their conservative counterparts, Beech concludes with thoughts on how the journey of Canadian churches is analogous to Israel in exile. The way Canadian churches navigate through post-Christendom may prove instructive for churches in other countries facing similar challenges.

Many of the challenges of Global Christianity have been experienced before in a similar form in the past. Gordon Heath examines the specter of the Armenian Genocide through the eyes of the Canadian Protestant press. Heath's contribution to this book is timely given the centenary commemoration of the Armenian genocide in 2015. Like Beech, he draws a strong line between local and global concerns. He also provides a sobering case study to buttress Sauer's concerns. Heath provides convincing evidence that the press documented the genocide and used it to urge Canada and its allies to decisively defeat Germany and Turkey. Wrestling with the question of whether the churches did "enough in response to the genocide," he concludes that, while the churches' support for the war effort was good in that it was partly motivated by a desire to end the genocide, they were naive to think that empires and nations would act solely on the basis of ethical considerations.

Peter Althouse and Michael Wilkinson pick up on the global trend towards charismatic expressions of faith. They begin by examining the history and nature of "soaking prayer" from its origins in the Toronto Airport Christian Fellowship to the Catch the Fire World ministry. Then they develop the connection between receiving love (the object of soaking prayer) and mission. Their understanding of love is built upon Pitirim Sorokin's attempt to examine love empirically, and on Christian scholars' building on his work to develop a model of "Godly love." This love is an integral component of mission; when it is missing, mission becomes nothing more than a performance. The Father's divine love, not human striving, is what drives Charismatic renewal and mission.

Finally, John H. Issak, David K. Tarus, and Seongho Kang share their firsthand insights into Christianity in their homelands. Issak gives a harrowing account of persecuted Christians in contemporary Iraq, providing impetus to Sauer's call for solidarity with them. It also supplies an opportunity to compare contemporary responses to persecution to Heath's account of how Canadian Christians responded to the persecution of fellow believers in the past. Tarus gives a personal account of the need for Christian

Introduction

leadership in Kenya and of the various challenges these leaders must face. He ends on a fitting note for this work: with hope for his people in spite of the challenges that beset them. Kang wrestles with the rise and fall of Christianity's cultural clout in Korea. He calls on Korean Protestant churches to set aside competitive behavior in favor of focusing on living in a way that is consistent with the faith they profess.

Bibliography

Cavanaugh, William T. *Theopolitical Imagination: Discovering the Liturgy as a Political Act in an Age of Global Consumerism*. 2002. Reprint, New York: T. & T. Clark, 2011.

Fletcher, Richard. *The Barbarian Conversion: From Paganism to Christianity*. Berkeley: University of California Press, 1999.

"Free Church Ministers in Anglican Pulpits. Dr. Temple's Call: The South India Scheme." *The Guardian*, 26 May 1943.

Hanciles, Jehu J. *Beyond Christendom: Globalization, African Migration, and the Transformation of the West*. Maryknoll, NY: Orbis, 2008.

Hastings, Adrian. *The Construction of Nationhood: Ethnicity, Religion and Nationalism*. Cambridge: Cambridge University Press, 1997.

Hiebert, Paul G. *Anthropological Reflections on Missiological Issues*. Grand Rapids: Baker, 1994.

———. "Metatheology: The Step beyond Contextualization." In *Reflection and Projection: Missiology at the Threshold of 2001*, edited by Hans Kasdorf and Klaus W. Müller, 383–95. Bad Liebenzell: Verlag der Liebenzeller Mission, 1988.

Hylson-Smith, Kenneth. *To the Ends of the Earth: The Globalization of Christianity*. London: Paternoster, 2007.

Jenkins, Philip. *The Next Christendom: The Coming of Global Christianity*. 3rd ed. Oxford: Oxford University Press, 2011.

Kalu, Ogbu U. "Globalization and Mission in the Twenty-first Century." In *Mission after Christendom: Emergent Themes in Contemporary Mission*, edited by Ogbu U. Kalu et al., 25–42. Louisville: Westminster John Knox, 2010.

Law, Stephen. *Humanism: A Very Short Introduction*. Oxford: Oxford University Press, 2011.

Lewis, C. S. *Surprised by Joy: The Shape of My Early Life*. Orlando: Houghton Mifflin Harcourt, 1966.

Murray, Stuart. *Post-Christendom: Church and Mission in a Strange New World (after Christendom)*. Carlisle: Paternoster, 2004.

Netland, Harold A. "Introduction: Globalization and Theology Today." In *Globalizing Theology: Belief and Practice in an Era of World Christianity*, edited by Craig Ott and Harold A. Netland, 14–34. Grand Rapids: Baker Academic, 2006.

Pocock, Michael, Gailyn Van Rheenen, and Douglas McConnell. *The Changing Face of World Missions: Engaging Contemporary Issues and Trends*. Encountering Mission. Grand Rapids: Baker Academic, 2005.

Porter, Andrew. *Religion versus Empire? British Protestant Missionaries and Overseas Expansion, 1700–1914*. Manchester: Manchester University Press, 2004.

Sanneh, Lamin. *Encountering the West: Christianity and the Global Cultural Process: The African Dimension*. Maryknoll, NY: Orbis, 1993.

Stanley, Brian. "Christianity and the End of Empire." In *Mission, Nationalism, and the End of Empire*, edited by Brian Stanley, 1–12. Grand Rapids: Eerdmans, 2003.

Tiénou, Tite. "Christian Theology in an Era of World Christianity." In *Globalizing Theology: Belief and Practice in an Era of Word Christianity*, edited by Craig Ott and Harold A. Netland, 37–51. Grand Rapids: Baker Academic, 2006.

Vanhoozer, Kevin J. ""One Rule to Rule Them All?" Theological Method in an Era of World Christianity." In *Global Theology: Belief and Practice in an Era of World Christianity*, edited by Craig Ott and Harold A. Netland, 85–126. Grand Rapids: Baker Academic, 2006.

Walls, Andrew. "Ecumenical Missiology in Anabaptist Perspective." *Mission Focus: Annual Review* 13 (2005) 191–98.

2

Changes and Trends in Global Christianity

Philip Jenkins

Not long ago, Christians were convinced that their faith was identified with Europe, and with Europe's possessions beyond the sea. Other religions might exist in these regions, but as guests, welcome or otherwise. Consciously or not, many Christians would have echoed the words of English travel writer Samuel Purchas, back in 1625:

> Europe is taught the way to scale Heaven, not by Mathematical principles, but by Divine veritie. Jesus Christ is their way, their truth, their life; who hath long since given a Bill of Divorce to ingratefull Asia where hee was born, and Africa the place of his flight and refuge, and is become almost wholly and only Europaean. For little doe we find of this name in Asia, lesse in Africa, and nothing at all in America, but later Europaean gleanings. Here are his Scriptures, Oratories, Sacraments, Ministers, Mysteries.[1]

Europe, he was saying, was synonymous with the Christian faith and, presumably, would remain so. If that analysis ever was true, it has long since ceased to be so. Our traditional concept of the Christian world as a predominantly white and Euro-American world—of Western Christianity in fact—is no longer the norm. This fact has vast implications for notions of church and for mission.

---

1. Purchas, *Hakluytus Posthumus*, 1:251.

The Globalization of Christianity

Shifting Numbers

I wish to tell a very simple story, but one that has complex consequences. Briefly, I will describe what has happened to the number and distribution of Christian believers worldwide over the past century or so, and how it has changed. I will then explore some of the implications of this change.

It is indeed a simple story. In the year 1900, about one-third of the world's people were Christians, and that proportion remains more or less unchanged today. Moreover, if we project our estimate forward to the year 2050, that proportion should still be about one third. The Christian proportion of the world's population therefore seems strikingly stable.

In other ways, though, the changes are far more striking. For one thing, the vast increase of global population means that the number of Christians has grown steeply in absolute terms. Global population in 1900 stood at 1.62 billion, compared to 6.9 billion today, and probably rising to 9.2 billion by 2050. As a result, the number of Christians alive today is about four times greater than what it was in 1900. Just by retaining a constant share of the world's population, then—that constant third—Christian numbers have swollen at a rate unimaginable to most eras of Christian history.

Far more significant is the geographical distribution of these believers, which is sketched in Table 1, based on the extraordinarily valuable resources supplied by the World Christian Database (WCD). As I will explain below, I have some reservations about the numbers provided for certain regions, but as a broad guide to the overall picture, the Database is reliable.

Table 1

The Changing Distribution of Christian Believers

Number of Christians in millions

Source: World Christian Database, http://www.worldchristiandatabase.org/wcd/

	1900	1970	2010	2050
Africa	10	143	493	1,031
Asia	22	96	352	601
North America	79	211	286	333
Latin America	62	270	544	655

Changes and Trends in Global Christianity

	1900	1970	2010	2050
EUROPE	381	492	588	530
OCEANIA	5	18	28	38
TOTAL	558	1,230	2,291	3,188

The most important trend we notice from these figures is, of course, the precipitous relative decline of North America and Europe as Christian heartlands. This does not mean that Christian numbers in these regions have declined, quite the contrary. Rather, these religious blocs have been overwhelmed by the relative growth of Christian numbers elsewhere, above all in those regions that have, since the 1980s, been known as the Global South—that is, the continents of Africa, Asia, and Latin America. According to the evidence presented by the WCD, between 1900 and 2010 the number of Christians in Europe grew by 29 percent, a substantial figure. In Africa, however, the absolute number of recorded believers grew in the same period by an incredible 4,930 percent. The comparable growth in Latin America was 877 percent. The growth for particular denominations was even more startling. During the twentieth century, Africa's Catholic population grew from 1.9 million to 130 million—an increase of 6,708 percent.

Two different processes are at work here. One is the growth of Christianity in some regions of the world at the expense of other faiths, above all of traditional or primal religions. This was most marked in Africa, where the Christian proportion of the continental population grew during the twentieth century from about 10 percent of the whole to around 46 percent. No less significant, however, was the spectacular increase of populations in the Global South. While European fertility rates remained stable or declined, the rates remained very high elsewhere in the world. In Latin America, the steep growth in Christian numbers is entirely due to population change. A continent that was already in 1900 almost wholly Christian (at least in terms of notional allegiance) simply acquired far more people.

The demographic change is even more marked in Africa, which in 1900 had perhaps 100 million people. That number passed the billion mark by 2005, and by 2050 the number could reach anywhere from 2 to 2.25 billion. Just to take one example, in the lands that would become Kenya, the population in 1900 was a mere one million, but that figure has now swollen to around 40 million, in little over a century. By 2050, Kenya could have

80 million people or more. In 1900, there were three Europeans for every African; by 2050, there should be three Africans for every European.

Not only were there far more Africans, but a much larger share of them were Christian. In consequence, the absolute number of African believers soared, from just 10 million in 1900 to 500 million by 2015 or so, and (if projections are correct) to an astonishing billion by 2050. Put another way, the number of African Christians in 2050 will be almost twice as large as the total figure for all Christians alive anywhere in the globe back in 1900.

Twentieth-century Christianity was decidedly a Euro-American faith. Combining Christian numbers in Europe and North America, these continents accounted for 82 percent of all believers in 1900, and even by 1970, that figure had fallen only to 57 percent. Since that point however, change has been very marked. Today, Euro-American Christians make up 38 percent of the worldwide total, and that figure could reach a mere 27 percent by 2050.

Actually, even those figures gravely understate the scale of the change, because the Christians listed as "European" or "North American" today include large communities from the Global South. By 2050, for instance, perhaps a quarter of the people of the USA will have roots in Latin America, and 50 or 60 million Americans will claim a Mexican heritage. Another 8 percent of Americans will have Asian ancestry, and usually those communities—Korean, Chinese, Vietnamese—have strong Christian elements. In Europe also, those enduring Christian populations will include sizable immigrant communities—African, Asian, and Afro-Caribbean. In 2050, therefore, even our "Euro-American" Christians will include Congolese believers living in Paris, Chinese in Vancouver, Koreans in Los Angeles, and Nigerians almost anywhere.

If we envisage the Christianity of the mid-twenty-first century, then at least in numerical terms, we have to think of a faith located much nearer the equator. Again according to WCD statistics, by far the largest share of the world's Christian population in 2050 will be African, with 32 percent of the global total. South Americans will make up 21 percent of the whole, a number that grows if we include people of Latino origin in North America. In short, well over half of all Christians alive in 2050 will be either African or Latin American. When we recall the distribution of Christians as recently as 1970, that is an incredible global change to occur in just two or three generations.

Reasons for Caution

I should explain here why I have raised some flags about accepting the WCD figures at face value. In Table 2, I list the world's largest Christian communities according to that source.

Table 2

The Largest Christians Populations 2010

Source: World Christian Database, http://www.worldchristiandatabase.org/wcd/

Nation	Number of Christians in Millions
USA	260
Brazil	177
China	115
Russia	115
Mexico	106
Philippines	84
Nigeria	72
D. R. Congo	65
Germany	58
India	58
Britain	50
Ethiopia	50

Two problems arise, illustrating the methodological difficulty of quantifying faith. In the case of Britain, for instance, the estimated figure of fifty million basically reflects every resident of the country not openly identified with some other religion. It certainly suggests nothing about actual Christian practice or commitment, or even the number of people who might admit to some kind of Christian identification, however lukewarm, in a survey. I would suggest, therefore, that the WCD exaggerates the number of Christian believers to be found in traditionally Christian countries that historically supported state churches, which particularly affects our sense of the level of Christian belief in Europe. However much Europe's importance in the Christian world has fallen over the past century, the WCD statistics actually understate this decline.

Equally problematic are the WCD estimates for countries where Christianity is strictly regulated or regarded with widespread suspicion by government or rival religious communities. Nobody doubts that countries like India and China have sizable Christian populations over and above what is portrayed by the official statistics of those nations. But how large are these shadow populations? Many observers would be suspicious of the very large Christian populations implied for China (115 million) and India (58 million). In India, for instance, official government data suggest a Christian population of around 23 million, which everyone knows to be an underestimate. Millions of Christians, especially among the poor, are nervous about openly admitting their faith in the face of potential persecution from fundamentalist Hindu groups. But a consensus of informed estimates puts India's real Christian population at around 40 million, rather than 58 million. Chinese data are even more open to speculation, and the WCD number of 115 million stands at the summit of likely estimates. I personally would place the probable number of Chinese Christians well below that, perhaps at a half of the WCD figure. I may well be wrong, but in this matter, neither I nor the scholars of the WCD really have any firm data on which to rely.

If the WCD figure for present-day adherents is inflated, then so are all projections for coming decades. These numbers in particular raise major difficulties for projecting Christian strength in Asia in years to come. The projected number of Asian Christians in 2050—over 600 million—may well be a considerable over-estimate. As I said, however, I do not have more solid evidence on which to base a rival figure.

Comparing Islam

In another area too, caution is justified. Let us assume that the numerical growth of Christianity really is as spectacular as it appears to be. Is this so spectacular that we should be speaking in terms of the miraculous, of a New Pentecost?

Actually, a comparison with Islamic growth in the same period is instructive, and should encourage a degree of modesty in the claims we make. Both religions have acquired vastly more adherents in the past century, but in some ways, Muslims have significantly outpaced Christians.

Changes and Trends in Global Christianity

When considered as a share of global population, Christian numbers have proved strikingly stable over the past century. I have already remarked on the "Constant Third." In the year 1900, about one-third of the world's people were Christians; that proportion remains more or less unchanged today, and it should remain true in the year 2050. But if we look at Muslim numbers in the same terms, as a share of the world's people, then that religion has enjoyed a far more impressive surge. In 1900, the 200 to 220 million Muslims then living comprised some 12 or 13 percent of humanity, compared to 22.5 percent today, and a projected figure of 27.3 percent by 2050. Put another way, Christians in 1900 outnumbered Muslims by 2.8 to 1. Today the figure is 1.5 to 1, and by 2050 it should be 1.3 to 1. Put another way, there are four times as many Christians alive as there were in 1900; but over the same period, Muslims have grown at least seven-fold.

So how can Christian numbers be exploding, but still be left so far behind Muslims in the rate of expansion? A large part of the answer lies in differential demographics, namely that some parts of the world are growing much faster than others. Briefly, European numbers have been growing very slowly indeed in comparison with those of Africa, Asia, and Latin America, and that is very good news indeed for a faith based chiefly in Asia and Africa, as Islam was historically. So yes, let us be awed and inspired by the rate of Christian growth worldwide; but we should never forget that the change is part of a broader global reorientation.

What the Change Means

If we confine our attention to Christianity alone, what are the implications of the great Southward shift? If the world's Christian population was simply being redistributed according to different geographic or ethnic patterns, that would be a matter of minor significance, a factoid perhaps, but not a change of real substance. However, the kinds of Christianity that are emerging and growing have very distinct characteristics from what the Euro-American world regards as familiar or mainstream. As we will see, the newer kinds of Christianity are strongly charismatic in tone, presenting a very different image from the "mainline" faith of North America or Europe.

The reasons for this difference are open to debate. Some observers might explain the ecstatic and charismatic nature of the newer churches in terms of the older and hitherto dominant cultures in regions of Christian growth, for instance the continuing impact of traditional and primal faiths in Africa. Other differences derive from the very fact of newness. As sociologists of religion have long known, new and emerging religious bodies tend to have particular characteristics, which mark them as sects rather than as churches. Neither of these terms, I hasten to add, has any derogatory sense, rather they are employed as a convenient label for a package of beliefs and characteristics. Sects, generally, tend to be more passionate and enthusiastic about their faith, more charismatic in tone, with a greater sense of the potential for miraculous intervention. They also encourage stronger lay and non-clerical involvement. The "sect" model does include many of the features commonly attributed to rising new churches whether in Africa, Asia, or Latin America.

But whatever the reasons, newer churches—and the churches that will increasingly dominate the global ecclesiastical scene—tend to focus on certain key issues of belief, theology, and practice, which set them apart from the older bodies of the Global North. In very general terms, I will sketch some of the key differences, which will probably become ever more salient in Christian thought in the coming decades. I am not suggesting that these characteristics enjoy some kind of geographical privilege, that they exist in Africa not Europe. I can easily point to European or US churches that share many of these same issues and features. My concern is in identifying the mainstream of belief and concern in respective regions.

Critical Themes

With that caveat in mind, I identify certain pressing theological questions that arise from the global shift in Christian faith. I will touch briefly on issues that I have discussed at greater length in my other writings, and which have also been addressed by such excellent scholars as Lamin Sanneh, Mark Noll, and John Allen.[2]

Charismatic Faith

As noted earlier, any observation of the fastest growing churches across the Global South stresses their charismatic quality.[3] They preach messages

---

2. See Jenkins, *Next Christendom*; Jenkins, *New Faces of Christianity*; Sanneh, *Whose Religion*; Sanneh, *Disciples of All Nations*; Noll, *New Shape*; Noll and Nystrom, *Clouds of Witnesses*; Allen, *Future Church*.

3. See, for example, Sanneh, *Disciples of All Nations*, 163–84.

that, to the familiar Western mainline churches, appear simplistically charismatic, not to mention visionary and apocalyptic. In this thought-world, prophecy is an everyday reality, while faith-healing, exorcism, and dream-visions are all fundamental parts of religious sensibility. This does not necessarily mean that these newer bodies belong to one of the historic Pentecostal denominations, but rather that they act in similar ways, whatever their polity or church labels. This is true of Anglicans and even Catholics, as well as Baptists and Presbyterians. The supreme challenge for Christian theology in the coming decades is the rediscovery of pneumatology, the theory of the workings of the Holy Spirit, and this task will span churches and denominations.

Deliverance and Spiritual Warfare

If there is a single critical marker distinguishing the Christianity of the modern West from the New Testament world, it is the basic belief in the supernatural character of evil, which is manifested equally in sickness, repression, wickedness, and compulsiveness. The North-South divide is not absolute, and some Euro-American Christians accept theories of the diabolic and demonic, of supernatural warfare, and spiritual healing. Yet most Northern-world Christians share the bemusement, the mockery, with which the more secular-minded regard such manifestations. For post-Enlightenment Christians in the West, the demonic elements in the New Testament mean so little that they are scarcely even an embarrassment anymore. Many Westerners read over such passages and attribute them to a long-departed stage of scientific development. Yet the supernatural approach certainly harks back to the ancient roots of Christianity.

To read the Gospels is to make the intimate acquaintance of demons and demonic forces. Arguing for a social justice approach to Christianity, Jim Wallis rightly points out that excising references to "the poor" leaves very little of the biblical text intact. But by the same principle, precious little is left of the New Testament after we purge all mentions of angels, demons, and spirits. Shorn of healing and miraculous cures, the four Gospels would be a slim pamphlet indeed. Large sections of the new Christianity assume a spiritual universe quite different from the view of mainline Western churches.

Healing

Demonology is thus credible for African and Asian churches in a way it can scarcely be for most educated Westerners, and so are ideas of exorcism and healing. Unless we appreciate the central role of healing, we can hardly understand the shape of modern Christianity globally. The emphasis on health and healing is not going to go away anytime soon, given the pervasive character of sickness in developing societies. Worse, hospital facilities there are so crowded and unhygienic that they deter many from seeking formal medical assistance, however bad their situation. This puts a premium on institutions that provide healing through spiritual means, a mission that is absolutely central to the fastest-growing churches of Africa, Latin America, and the Pacific Rim communities. Such churches offer a culture of spectacle through great healing missions, revivals, and miracle crusades. Other institutions win supporters by dispensing medical services through volunteer doctors and paramedics, a ministry undertaken by Christian missionaries and by fundamentalist mosques. I quote the sermon of a leader of the West African Mosama Disco Christo Church, who tells his followers, "We are all here in this church because we have found healing here. But for this church, the great majority of us here assembled would not be alive today. That is the reason why we are here."[4] The point is so obvious in Africa, and so very strange to Western believers. Even African Mennonites are, of course, a healing church. How could they be otherwise?

Notions of healing and exorcism are anything but new in the Christian context: witness two thousand years of saints' lives and tales of miraculous shrines. But in the past half century, these ideas have returned to the forefront of Christian expansion as broadly charismatic and Pentecostal churches have experienced the most explosive growth worldwide. And instead of being confined to inspiring stories of holy heroes in ages past, healing is now the expectation of ordinary believers in every tin-roofed Pentecostal church.

John Allen has ably explored this change in the context of the Roman Catholic Church, which is still the world's largest religious institution. While the Roman Catholic Church has always regarded itself as "One, Holy, Catholic, and Apostolic," Allen sees the coming Southward-weighted institution as "Global, Uncompromising, Pentecostal, and Extroverted."[5] That a

---

4. Pobee, "Healing," 248.
5. Allen, *Future Church*, 432.

Southern-rooted Catholic Church will be charismatic or Pentecostal seems almost inevitable. Whether it can be Pentecostal enough to retain the loyalty of its members—sufficiently flexible to admit the power of religious gifts outside the traditional hierarchical structures—is an open question.

Denominations and Labels

When Americans ask me the most important thing they need to know about Christian life in Africa, for example, I always reply that first and foremost, they need to abandon their familiar assumptions about ecclesiastical parties and denominations. Western observers of global South Christianity often try, unsuccessfully, to impose familiar categories upon it, familiar divisions between left and right, between conservative and liberal, between otherworldly charismatics and this-worldly social activists. Countless American examples demonstrate the flaws in this analysis, but in the churches of the global South, the division makes even less sense. Christianity only makes sense as a faith that heals—heals the body, the soul, and the spirit, as well as healing society and community. Deliverance and liberation are one. Similarly, forms of behavior and practice span denominations in ways that seem strange in a Western context, so that concepts like "evangelical," "liturgical," "catholic," and "charismatic" can be combined in ways that seem utterly bizarre to mainline Westerners.

Minorities

For many centuries, Western Christians have lived in societies virtually lacking any form of religious competition. Some have succeeded in forming an accommodation with tiny Jewish minorities, while others, of course, have failed miserably in this endeavor. The main rivals for the loyalty of the faithful have long been secular movements, whether socialist or Communist, liberal or fascist. Often too, Christians have enjoyed political power, allowing them to shape the wider society as they saw fit. Their majority status was long unquestioned and unchallenged.

In the Global South, of course, Christianity emerges in quite different settings, against the background of ancient and deeply established rival faiths. Christians must therefore learn to live as minorities, with all that implies for the constraints placed on overt evangelism and proselytizing. What happens when the main interlocutors in religious debate operate from assumptions quite different from those of secular critics, when the rivals assume as a given the existence and power of a personal God who intervenes directly in human affairs, and seek to clarify the nature of his revelation?

The central fact of African religious history during the twentieth century was the conversion of about half the continental population from animism or primal religions to Christianity and Islam: about 40 percent to Christianity, 10 percent to Islam. African Christians must, therefore, on a daily basis, negotiate their relationships to both animism and Islam, determining the acceptable limits of compromise. The process of determining the relationship to paganism is, of course, a story very familiar to scholars of the Early Church. The interaction with Islam poses quite different problems, which, if handled wrongly, can lead to serious bloodshed.

Asian Christians face problems scarcely less severe in their interactions with ancient literate faiths such as Buddhism, Confucianism, and Taoism. Believers wish to shape and protect a social space for themselves, preserving good relations while remaining steadfast against any temptation to syncretism. To determine how to do this, they must constantly draw on biblical examples and precedents.

Islam

Each of the rival faiths poses its particular issues and dangers, but perhaps none so much as Islam, which in its origins shares so many common assumptions with Christianity. Much modern scholarship suggests early forms of parallel development far closer than we might have suspected. Some see major survivals of Christian texts within the Quran itself, and trace Christian origins for many Muslim religious practices.

The question then remains as another pressing theological challenge of the new century: what is, and what should be, the relationship between Christianity and Islam? Is Islam a separate religion, as distinct from Christianity as Shinto or Hinduism, or are the two religions sisters separated at birth and raised in different family settings? Is Islam the offspring of the devil? Or is it a Christian heresy that could somehow be brought back into the fold? And the Quran: is it legitimately a prophetic Scripture, revealed by God? Multiculturalism might demand accepting such a position, but if you go so far, what prevents you from going all the way and becoming a

Muslim? At what point must a desire to coexist with another world religion give way to the urgent necessity to draw and enforce lines of orthodoxy?

And what about Christian evangelism toward Muslims, assuming that this is even a practical possibility? Are Muslims members of a distinct religion, in need of receiving the Christian revelation, or do they already possess the truth in sufficient measure to make such efforts unnecessary and undesirable? Many Christian churches in Europe and North America, especially of liberal inclination, have already decided against the propriety of evangelizing Jews, since to do so would be to condemn the Jewish Covenant as invalid and obsolete. But do Muslims too have a valid path to God?

Different Ways of Reading the Bible

In other ways too, Christians in the new churches must once again ask some ancient questions, reopening debates that the West thought were long settled. Some of the most critical ones concern the correct way of reading the Bible itself. Any acquaintance with African or Asian Christianity soon indicates the pervasive importance of the Bible and of biblical stories. The Bible has found a congenial home among communities who identify with the social and economic realities it portrays no less than the political environments in which Christians find themselves. Cultures that readily identify with biblical worldviews find it easier to read the Bible not just as historical fact, but as relevant instruction for daily conduct.

Reading the Bible through "Southern" eyes helps Western believers appreciate the Bible as an immediate contemporary document, and makes it hard to see the Bible as simply a historical text. I do not claim that contemporary Africans or Asians have received prophetic insight that allows them the power of precisely correct interpretation of the first century Mediterranean world. Often, their readings are probably wide of the mark, and they wrongly apply modern understandings to the ancient world. But in many instances, these contemporary readings are deeply enlightening. And the more immediately one understands the biblical world, the easier it becomes to accept the authority of the text. In the words of one liberal African theologian, Kenya's Musimbi Kanyoro, "Those cultures which are far removed from biblical culture risk reading the Bible as fiction."[6] How strange: reading the Bible as fiction!

---

6. Kanyoro, "Reading the Bible," 20.

Writing of contemporary Central America, novelist Francisco Goldman remarks:

> Guatemala certainly feels biblical. Sheep, swine, donkeys, serpents—these are everywhere, as are centurions, all manner of wandering false prophets, pharisees, lepers and whores. The poor, rural, mainly Mayan landscape has an aura of the miraculous. . . . [It] is the perfect backdrop for religious parables about fields both barren and fertile, fruits and harvests, hunger and plenty.[7]

Across Africa and Asia, millions of modern readers know roads where a traveler is likely to be robbed and left for dead, without much hope of intervention by official agencies. They relate to accounts of streets teeming with the sick. They understand that a poor woman who loses a tiny sum of money would search frantically for coins that could allow her children to eat that night. In many countries, readers appreciate the picture of the capricious rich man, who offers hospitality on one occasion, but on another day demands payment of exorbitant debts and obligations, and who must not on any account be offended. Today, however, the person would not be a generic magnate or Hellenistic princeling, but the corrupt official of a ruling party.

The Old Testament

Specifically, for these "new eyes," the relationship between different portions of the Bible is an issue of lively discussion. For many American Christians, who may love the stories of the ancient Hebrew world, it is all too obvious that these arise from an utterly different social and economic setting, which is of limited practical relevance to a modern society. In contrast, it is precisely the Old Testament world that speaks in contemporary tones to many African and Asian Christians. I quote for instance Madipoane Masenya, a feminist liberal theologian from contemporary South Africa: "If present day Africans still find it difficult to be at home with the Old Testament, they might need to watch out to see if they have not lost their Africanness in one way or the other."[8] Could a comparable observation conceivably be made of contemporary Europeans or North Americans?

---

7. Goldman, "Gospel according to Matthew," 210.
8. Masenya, "Wisdom and Wisdom Converge," 145.

Cultural affinities with the biblical world lead African and Asian Christians to a deep affection for the Old Testament as their story, their book. In Africa particularly, Christians have long been excited by the obvious cultural parallels that exist between their own societies and those of the Hebrew Old Testament, especially the world of the patriarchs. While the majority of modern Africans have no direct experience of nomadism or polygamy, at least they can relate to the kind of society in which such practices were commonplace. Many are also thoroughly familiar with notions of blood sacrifice, of atonement through blood.

If the Old Testament world makes sense to modern Africans, if they see it as a recognizable parallel to their own world, this makes it much easier to accept the moral and even legal prescriptions laid down in its books. Not only does the Bible carry special authority as a divinely inspired text, but this respect must be paid to larger portions of the text than would be customary for many Northern-world Christians. If not quite a different book, the Bible of the South is perhaps a good deal larger than its Northern counterpart.

Conclusion

I have outlined these implications in the briefest possible terms, and we could easily think of many other consequences of the current global shift, but in conclusion, let me draw just two points. First, the current changes in Christianity are unprecedented in scale, and might even dwarf the revolutionary transformation that we call the Reformation. Second, any understanding of the current changes demands the mastery of a wide range of disciplines, in the study of society and economics as much as theology, but perhaps more than anything, it demands a strong sense of history. After all, so many of the "new" questions that will face the churches in coming decades are anything but new. Rather, they were debates and controversies deeply familiar to the most primitive church, and in many subsequent eras. Without knowing that history, that prehistory, we will be doomed to a constant reinvention of the wheel.

Bibliography

Allen, John L., Jr. *The Future Church: How Ten Trends Are Revolutionizing the Catholic Church*. New York: Doubleday, 2009.

Goldman, Francisco. "The Gospel according to Matthew." In *Revelations: Personal Responses to the Books of the Bible*, 203–14. London: Canongate, 2005.

Jenkins, Philip. *The New Faces of Christianity: Believing the Bible in the Global South*. New York: Oxford University Press, 2006.

———. *The Next Christendom: The Coming of Global Christianity*. 3rd ed. Oxford: Oxford University Press, 2011.

Kanyoro, Musimbi. "Reading the Bible from an African Perspective." *The Ecumenical Review* 51, no. 1 (1999) 18–24.

Masenya, Madipoane. "Wisdom and Wisdom Converge: Selected Old Testament and Northern Sotho Proverbs." In *Interpreting the Old Testament in Africa: Papers from the International Symposium on Africa and the Old Testament in Nairobi, October 1999*, edited by Mary N. Getui, Knut Holter, and Victor Zinkuratire, 133–46. New York: Peter Lang, 2001.

Noll, Mark A. *The New Shape of World Christianity: How American Experience Reflects Global Faith*. Downers Grove, IL: IVP Academic, 2009.

Noll, Mark A., and Carolyn Nystrom. *Clouds of Witnesses: Christian Voices from Africa and Asia*. Downers Grove, IL: InterVarsity, 2011.

Pobee, John S. "Healing: An African Christian Theologian's Perspective." *International Review of Mission* 83, no. 329 (1994) 247–55.

Purchas, Samuel. *Hakluytus Posthumus, or, Purchas His Pilgrimes: Contayning a History of the World in Sea Voyages and Lande Travells by Englishmen and Others*. 20 vols. Glasgow: James MacLehose & Sons, 1905.

Sanneh, Lamin O. *Disciples of All Nations: Pillars of World Christianity*. Oxford Studies in World Christianity. Oxford: Oxford University Press, 2008.

———. *Whose Religion Is Christianity?: The Gospel beyond the West*. Grand Rapids: Eerdmans, 2003.

World Christian Database. Online: http://www.worldchristiandatabase.org/wcd/ (accessed September 2012).

3

New Models of Ministry in Canada as a Response to the Decline of Western Christianity

LEE BEACH

THE RE-ORDERING OF CHRISTIANITY's locus of power and the "new Christendom"[1] is a reflection of many things, one of which is the decline of Christianity in Canada. The global change being experienced by Christianity is having particular local effects on this once highly "Christian" nation. As in many other Western nations, the churches, both Catholic and Protestant, are trying to determine how they can effectively navigate their way through the immense cultural change they are facing, and the concomitant social dislocation.

Canada was once a nation where the majority of the citizens not only identified themselves as either Protestant or Catholic on the census (as the majority still do), but also showed up to worship in large numbers on Sunday. However, in recent decades, Canada has experienced a fairly consistent decline in church attendance and people identifying themselves as Christian on the census.[2] While a thorough exploration of the many factors contributing to this decline lies beyond the scope of this chapter, some of them include the change in immigration patterns, the rise of secularism, and the growing affluence of the population.[3] The result is that the church

---

1. For a full exploration of this phenomenon, see Jenkins, *Next Christendom*, 2002.

2. See Bibby, *Beyond the Gods and Back*, 44; Bibby, *Emerging Millennials*, 176.

3. There is substantial discussion about the term "secularism," both its meaning and the process of it. For example, see Marshall, *Secularizing the Faith*; Taylor, *Secular Age*.

has increasingly moved from near the center of culture to somewhere near the margins. Today in Canada, new models of ministry are emerging that are seeking to help the church reorient and contextualize itself effectively in the new order of things. This chapter presents some of the key models that are emerging and offers a brief analysis of their potential effectiveness. More specifically, it will briefly look at current Canadian attitudes toward the church. These attitudes indicate that the immediate future shows few signs of reversal from the decline that has become the longstanding trend for the church in Canada and other countries in the Western world. I will then look at some of the key models that are emerging and show how they are a response to both traditional forms of ministry and to the new cultural realities that are a part of Canadian life. Finally, I will offer a brief analysis of these models and the potential contributions that they are making, and consider some questions that this analysis raises about their long-term effectiveness.

While there is much to be encouraged about in the development of global Christianity, many in Canada would say that there is not much for the Canadian church to rejoice about when one looks at the macro-trends. However, what is happening in Canada in response to these trends is a part of the story of global Christianity, and the Canadian churches' re-envisioning of themselves can help inform the journey of the church in other Western nations as well.

Emerging Trends in Canadian Christianity

There are at least two key trends that must be considered in order to understand the place of the church in contemporary Canadian society. The first is that non-Christians are ambivalent about institutional religion and are simply not attending traditional churches. The research of Reginald Bibby, one of Canada's leading researchers on religion, offers some sobering statistics. Telling trends appear when one examines the ongoing research that he has done on young people from 1984 through to 2008. The following data reflect the response of his survey group of youth aged 15 to 19 to the question of their religious affiliation:

	1984	2008
ROMAN CATHOLIC	50%	32%
PROTESTANT	35%	13%
OTHER	3%	16%
NONE	12%	32%

Clearly a significant shift has taken place in these categories of religious identification over the past twenty-four years.[4] It is noteworthy that the percentage in the "other" category has risen exponentially, but perhaps what is most striking about this data is the dramatic shift seen in the comparison between those declaring themselves Protestants and those declaring themselves affiliated with no specific religious group. The numbers are essentially inverted as Protestant numbers have dropped and "none's" numbers have risen sharply. This does not bode well for the immediate future of the Protestant church, as it would seem that the trend is moving decidedly away from participation in that particular form of Christianity. That said, Catholic numbers are not much better and do not offer much encouragement either.

Bibby also offers the following statistics on Canadians' habits in terms of church attendance according to their age. In response to the statement, "I never attend church services," the following reflects the percentage of those who affirmed the statement.

Pre-Boomers (b. <1946) – 17%

Boomers (b. 1946–64) – 25%

Post-Boomers (b. >1965) – 24%

Millennials (b. 1989–93) – 47%[5]

Most striking here is the fact that almost half of those born between 1989 and 1993 (15 to 19 years old at the time of this survey) declare that they never attend church services. In response to an analysis of his own data Bibby wrote, "For years I have been saying that, for all the problems of

---

4. Bibby, *Emerging Millennials*, 176.

5. Ibid., 185.

organized religion in Canada, God has continued to do well in the polls; that's no longer the case."[6]

While this is admittedly only a small snapshot of the religious landscape in Canada today, it does offer an accurate depiction of the reality of the decline of Christianity and the changing place of the church in society. It also reflects the possibility that, in light of the response of the young people Bibby surveyed, the future will indeed be difficult for the churches.

The second trend is that Christians are disillusioned with the church and are either leaving or looking for alternative forms. Almost anyone familiar with the church context in Canada is aware that there is a growing dissatisfaction with the traditional institutional church. This dissatisfaction is resulting in an exodus from North American churches by those who are not necessarily giving up on the faith itself, but are taking a break from church as they know it. Julia Duin, religion editor for the *Washington Times*, chronicles this dissatisfaction in her book *Quitting Church*. Her research is based on polling research, interviews with experts and "average" Christians, and her personal experience, and her findings indicate that a significant number of Christians are leaving established churches. While her work focuses on Americans in particular, Duin's findings are reflected in Canadian Christianity. As in the United States, the mainline churches in Canada have been in decline for some time, but evangelical denominations had held steady and, in some cases, even grown. Duin notes that the decline has now also spread to evangelical churches. She writes, "Evangelicals, for a variety of reasons, are heading out of church—not all of them and not everywhere, but the trend is undeniable. Sunday mornings at church have become too banal, boring, or painful. Large groups of Christians are opting out of church because they find it impossible to stay."[7] She claims the irrelevance of the services, lack of genuine community, inability to change, and ongoing church conflict are the key reasons for this mass exodus. This is a striking conclusion, for it is not just that people are less inclined to become Christians and thus populate the church; it is also that those who claim to be Christians are becoming less inclined to attend the established church.[8]

---

6. Ibid., 166.

7. Duin, *Quitting Church*, 21.

8. Bibby explores this from a Canadian perspective in chapter 6 of *Beyond the Gods and Back*.

Emerging Models of Ministry in Canadian Christianity

In response to both of these trends new movements have emerged in the West. On the one hand, they are an attempt to reach an increasingly unchurched population, and, on the other hand, they are an attempt by Christians to find a more satisfying church experience than what they have become accustomed to. Often these new church experiences fall under the label "emerging churches" although that term has become increasingly nebulous due to overuse and the lack of clear definition as to exactly what constitutes an "emerging church." Nonetheless, it still retains its usefulness because it describes a type of church that is intentionally distinct from the traditional church. In addition to being an attempt to make Christianity relevant, the emerging church is also marked by a commitment to postmodernism in some form or other. For some practitioners in these new movements the entanglement with postmodernism is not a conscious choice, but many others make a conscious decision to employ postmodern ideals in their emerging ministry.

All of these new models are characterized by two streams that merge together. The first stream is methodological. All of these new movements demonstrate a commitment to practicing the faith differently than it has been practiced in traditional churches. These models, in varying degrees, offer very different ways of "doing church" than has been common in most institutional churches for the past number of decades, and even centuries. The other stream is theological. It is quite wrong to think of the emerging church as simply a matter of people wanting to "update" the liturgy, or make the service more contemporary. Along with different practices there is also a reconfiguring of the Christian faith taking place in many emerging movements. Some of the theological assumptions of the emergent church and how they contrast with more traditional assumptions will become apparent in the following exploration of these new models. While there are various new models to choose from, the following four offer a helpful overview of these new movements in contemporary Christianity.

New Models of Established Church Ministry

There are within the emerging movement numerous congregations that are trying to reinvent the worship service and reconfigure important aspects of congregational life by employing a variety of new or, in some cases, ancient forms. Some of these churches choose to transform public spaces by holding their worship services or church gatherings in places like coffee shops, storefronts, shopping malls, or old warehouses. This is often attached to a theology of Incarnation that understands the church to be a people who are to follow in the incarnational life of Jesus as he ventured into non-religious places to fulfill his mission to the world. Wherever they meet, such churches often incorporate into worship things like creative approaches to teaching, congregational interaction during the service, dance, visual arts, and several different genres of music. The service may include ancient elements of worship blended with very contemporary forms and it is not uncommon for the Lord's Supper to be a standard part of the service even in traditions where this has not normally been the case. Often there is a significant emphasis placed on the relational life of the members and on their life together as a community. This is coupled with the fact that most of these emerging congregations also place an emphasis on recapturing the missional nature of the church, and thus they seek to engage meaningfully with their immediate neighborhood and the world as a whole.

While the exact styles of these new models of church vary greatly, they are attuned to postmodernist sensibilities, culturally engaged, contemporary, sometimes avant-garde, usually informal, and relationally focused. They vary from traditional churches in their meeting places, their forms of worship, and their willingness to engage in creative ways with people outside of the church body.[9]

House Churches

House churches are groups of approximately six to thirty people who meet together, usually in someone's home. These churches emphasize simplicity and reject traditional church culture by doing away with a church building, multiple programs, and paid clergy. They focus on the basics of prayer, fellowship, learning, and evangelism. All are encouraged to participate in the gatherings by sharing their gifts, offering their insight into the topic being studied, praying for others, bringing refreshments, and participating in life together outside of the group meeting. In some cases a group may

---

9. For further exploration of the various forms that these new initiatives are taking, particularly in Canada, see Studebaker and Beach, "Emerging Churches in Post-Christian Canada."

grow large enough to plant new house churches. These churches remain associated with one another and form a network of house churches that can function together under some kind of loose leadership structure. These networks may meet all together for worship or mission projects either regularly or periodically.

For some, this movement is seen as a return to early Christianity when the church was largely established as a house church movement. It recaptures some of the simplicity and commitment to body life that seems to be reflected in the account in Acts of the first-century church. The smaller nature of these churches allows for meaningful relationships to be built and for focused mission to occur as was the case in the early church.[10]

Internet Church

What was once an obscure fringe movement in Christianity at the beginning of the twenty-first century has quickly emerged as a significant new model of ministry. For many people, virtual church is no longer considered an addendum to "real" church; for an increasing number, their experience with Jesus and his church via the internet is as real as anything they have known in the non-virtual world.

The internet church is no longer about blogging or a chat room devoted to discussing theological ideas. In its early stages, church on the internet consisted of churches streaming their worship services and posting Christian content on a website and inviting people to interact together about it. While these approaches remain as a means through which people participate in church life, recent technological advances can be applied in new ways to religious experience. New technologies are also opening up the possibility of new applications of these technologies to religious experience. An early example of this phenomenon has been *Second Life*, an internet site that invites people to literally live a "second life" by creating an avatar for themselves and engaging in life in the virtual world. Within *Second Life* there are many possibilities for engaging in church experiences that range from high Anglican services to free flowing charismatic gatherings. While sites such as this come and go in terms of their popularity and currency, such possibilities offer the participant the opportunity to engage in virtual worship and church community in a way that is highly contextualized for

10. For a helpful overview of the house church movement, see Zdero, *Global House Church Movement*.

people who have been raised in a world where life lived in the virtual world is equally as valid as life lived in the physical realm. Doug Estes, who is both a participant in and a writer about virtual Christianity, has defined the virtual church as a church that "is the confessing people gathered in a synthetic world," and further as "a virtually localized assembly of the people of God dwelling in meaningful community with the task of building the kingdom."[11] In his writing he legitimates this movement in contemporary Christianity and reminds us that it is not a fringe movement but an option that people are increasingly choosing as their preferred way of participating in Christian community and mission.

The internet church movement is a rapidly evolving phenomenon. It represents what may be the most fluid form of new church models as it, like the technology that supports it, changes constantly as participants constantly experiment with the possibilities that technology offers. Thus, the internet church captures a spirit of the age as it allows digital "natives," that is, people born and bred in the digital age, to engage in Christian spirituality in the virtual world. Yet because of its highly interactive nature it also boasts as one of its strengths the opportunity to experience the faith in a highly communal and egalitarian way that some would say is much more true to the early life of the church.[12]

New Monastics

The new monastic movement can be characterized as communities of people who move into a neighborhood and live together in a highly communal way. The chosen neighborhood is almost always an economically disadvantaged one where there are many apparent needs among the residents. Members of the new monastic community often live together in the same residence, share belongings, pool resources (including their income), and work together to care for their residence/home in order to experience true biblical community together with a vision of also serving the community into which they have moved.

While there is a definite desire to experience the reality of a simple life, depth of relational connection with others, and authentic spiritual community among these new monastic orders, they are primarily driven by a

---

11. Estes, *SimChurch*, 37.

12. For some sympathetic but critical engagement on virtual churches, see Campbell, "Congregation of the Disembodied."

New Models of Ministry in Canada

missional vision. This vision arises out of a Kingdom theology of incarnating Jesus in a specific place and time. Shane Claiborne, who is one of the more prominent participants in this movement, describes the activities of his incarnational community in South Philadelphia this way:

> We hang out with kids and help them with homework in our living room, and jump in open fire hydrants on hot summer days. We share food with folks who need it, and eat the beans and rice our neighbor Ms Sunshine makes for us. Folks drop in all day to say hi, have a safe place to cry, or get some water or a blanket . . . We run a community store out of our house. We call it the Gathering, and neighbors can come in and fill a grocery bag with clothes for a dollar or find a couch, a bed or a refrigerator.[13]

The new monastic movement represents a new model of church that, like the others discussed here, is an attempt to recapture the essence of the early church in a contemporary context. These new movements are oriented toward a postmodern, post-Christian context in that they tend to resist traditional, or what might be deemed as modernist, ideas about the church and instead embrace something that is understood to be more authentic, relational, open-minded, and connected to early Christianity. While none of these movements is exclusively Canadian they can all be found emerging on the landscape of current Canadian Christianity.[14]

CHARACTERIZING THESE NEW MOVEMENTS

While these movements are obviously quite diverse in the approach that they take in addressing the demise of Western Christendom, there are some characteristics they often share that make them distinct from more traditional approaches that have characterized church ministry in the past. Identifying these characteristics and contrasting them with traditional approaches may help to shine further light on what makes these new models qualitatively different from what has gone before. This summary is not meant to be pejorative toward either the traditional or emerging church. Its broad scope requires some generalizations, but that does not make it inaccurate in its description of contemporary and more traditional models of church ministry.

13. Claiborne, *Irresistible Revolution*, 122.
14. For further exploration of the New Monastic Movement, see Arpin-Ricci, *Cost of Community*; Bessenecker, *New Friars*.

Leadership

Traditionally, leadership has been hierarchical and patriarchal. Organizational charts reflect a top down approach to congregational leadership and the positions at the top of the structure are most often held by men. There is also a distinct line drawn between the clergy and laity in that clergy are seen as "professional" ministers while others occupy a lesser role as "volunteers." This distinction also gives the clergy a certain status within the life of the local congregation.

New models of church ministry in Canada tend to emphasize a more shared and egalitarian approach to leadership where organizational charts—if they even exist—are more flat and informal. Women are encouraged to participate fully in the leadership of the church, including the ranks of the clergy. Moreover, the distinction between clergy and the rest of the congregation is lessened by a clear acknowledgement that all are called to serve according to their gifts and passions. In many new models there is far less emphasis placed on the clergy, and those who may serve the church in a vocational way are not accorded special status within the life of the congregation.[15]

Worship Service

In more traditional models, the style of the worship service is presentational with an emphasis on what the person at the front of the congregation is doing. For example, at the center of the Protestant service is a sermon that is most often delivered by a "professional" minister.[16] In newer models the service is more participatory with various activities planned that invite people to interact with each other and/or with the person who may be presenting from the front. In certain models the teaching may still retain a place of prominence but that is usually tempered by the emphasis that is placed on inviting everyone to participate. In some new models, where their denominational tradition has been to place primary emphasis on the sermon, they are reconfiguring worship in order to emphasize liturgy and the Lord's Supper as the primary elements. Some churches employing these

---

15. For further reflection on this style of leadership in the church, see Morganthaler, "Leadership in a Flattened World."

16. This is of course not the case in some Protestant traditions where the emphasis is on the liturgy and the Lord's Supper. However, in many Protestant traditions this is a fair evaluation of how things work.

new models have shifted away from a denominational tradition that places primary emphasis on the sermon in order to emphasize liturgy and Lord's Supper as the primary elements.[17]

Discipleship Style

Older models of discipleship often emphasize the acquisition of knowledge as the key to one's development as a disciple of Jesus. This was characterized, particularly in Evangelicalism, by the discipleship materials that were produced by denominational offices, parachurch organizations, and publishing houses that emphasized inductive Bible study. This approach involved looking up Bible verses and filling in blanks or answering questions supplied in the lessons. Later materials took a slightly more discussion based approach but the idea was still that acquiring knowledge was the foundation for spiritual growth. This did not exclude other things like prayer, church attendance, service, and fellowship with other believers as practices essential to spiritual growth, but in most cases being a better disciple was rooted in knowing the right things.

New models tend to emphasize character development as key to faithful discipleship. This means that doing the right things is more important than knowing the right things. Character was important in former models, but in newer models, discipleship is rooted in helping people to understand what it means to live in obedience to the lordship of Jesus by embodying the principles of his teaching in the actual living of life. This, of course, necessitates actually knowing Jesus' teaching, but what is ultimately affirmed in newer approaches to ministry is people's living out Kingdom values rather than their knowledge of Scripture or ability to articulate correct doctrine.[18]

Evangelism

Traditionally, evangelism has been understood as a very church-centered enterprise epitomized by the evangelistic church service, at one time held on Sunday nights, and later held in the form of a "seeker" service on Sunday morning or other appropriate times throughout the weekend. In addition

17. For more reflection on the changing nature of worship in emerging church models, see Gibbs and Bolger, *Emerging Churches*, ch. 11.

18. An example of this kind of approach to disciple-making can be found in Frost, *Exiles*, especially ch. 3.

to this, evangelism was done by going door to door and inviting people to come to a Sunday service, or running a Sunday school bus ministry that picked children up in their neighborhood and took them to the church's Sunday School program, or it was accomplished by hosting some kind of program at the church that people would perceive as useful to their lives, be it a financial seminar, a parenting course, or a course designed to give unbelievers a place to explore the basics of the Christian faith. All of these approaches to reaching out were rooted in a local church program of one kind or another and the expressed goal was to save people's souls from the power and consequence of sin.

New models of ministry emphasize the need to be "missional" and incarnational. This means engaging naturally with the community that the church finds itself in through building relationships, serving in already established community programs, and/or creating programs that do not ask people to come to the church but rather facilitate the church going to people. Many of these initiatives revolve around issues of social action or social justice such as caring for the poor, meeting the needs of people who are disenfranchised, and developing programs that will lead to community improvement. Rather than stressing the salvation of souls, it is the advance of God's Kingdom that is important; then as people experience a taste of this Kingdom they will be drawn to enter it as followers of Jesus. The issue is not so much the salvation of the soul as it is bringing the Kingdom of God to bear on the world so that the deadening power of sin may be defeated by the power of Kingdom life.[19]

Doctrine and Beliefs

Traditional models of church in the evangelical tradition have been largely shaped by fundamentalism and its response to the emerging liberalism of the late nineteenth and early twentieth century. This was largely rooted in a fairly literal reading of the Bible and a commitment to specific doctrinal formulations, usually determined by a given church's denominational body. Determining who belonged to your group and who did not was largely based on whether or not they agreed with the specific doctrinal ideas that your group espoused.

---

19. Contemporary approaches such as these are reflected in various ways in Adeney, *Graceful Evangelism*; Stone, *Evangelism after Christendom*.

New models are often guided by a term like "generous orthodoxy," which indicates a less stringent approach to doctrine and an openness to varying views.[20] Such an approach is largely shaped by postmodernism and post-liberal theology. It is rooted in a narrative reading of Scripture, being comfortable with the mystery of God, and the idea that doctrinal formulations need to be held with humility since epistemological certainty is extremely elusive.

Approach to Culture

More established models of ministry tend to have a dualistic view of culture that sees a deep distinction between the church and the world. Their overall approach to the world around them recognizes that the church has to be "in the world" because of its evangelistic mandate, but beyond this missional imperative, secular culture is largely something that needs to be rejected, avoided, or kept at arm's length. The church and the world are separate entities and this separation is seen as an appropriate posture for the church to maintain.

New models adopt a more integrated philosophy of church and culture. The church is called to embrace the world in the same way that Jesus in his Incarnation became a full participant in the culture into which he came. The world, therefore, is not something to be avoided but something to participate in fully and enthusiastically as it is God's domain every bit as much as is the church. This embracing of culture brings about a blurring of the lines between the sacred and the secular. Rather than seeing most of the world as non-sacred and even sullied by sin, new initiatives in Christianity tend to see most of the world as sacred; in other words, God is present everywhere. The mandate of the church is to help bring out or accentuate the sacredness that is already present in the world by drawing attention to where God is in the midst of all forms of culture and cultural expression.[21]

These trends demonstrate at least two things. One is deconstructive in that some of the ways that the church is emerging in Canada and the West is a reaction against "traditional" church culture and approaches to ministry. The other is reconstructive in that it is an attempt to contextualize the Christian faith in a postmodern, post-Christian culture. These two driving

20. McLaren, *Generous Orthodoxy*.

21. For instance, see Henderson, Hunter, and Spinks, *Outsider Interviews*; Thomlinson, *Post-Evangelical*.

impulses invite an assessment of their potential contributions to the church and reflection on what potential deficiencies they bring to the development of a post-Christendom church.

Potential Contributions of New Models to the Canadian Church

Many of these new developments are offering significant changes to the established way of "doing" church in Canada and other Western countries as well. Whenever change is proposed and enacted it is bound to threaten established models of doing things and perhaps even those who have participated in the traditional ways for some time. If there is hesitation among those who identify with established paradigms of church ministry to embrace some of these changes it is important to reflect on what the potential benefits to the church may be if they are to allow these emerging trends to direct the future life of the church in Canada and other parts of the West. The following possibilities present some the potential contributions that new church movements are making to Christianity in the Western world today.

An Attempt to Re-focus on the Person of Jesus and Early Christianity

These new models, almost without exception, seek to focus on the Jesus of the Gospels and the life of the early church as depicted in the book of Acts. Certain streams of these emerging movements even reject what they believe is an overemphasis on Pauline theology in the development of the Western church. Instead, they seek to rediscover the person of Jesus, his message, and the early church's appropriation of that message, in order to put these things at the forefront of their theology and practice. The spirit behind this restructuring of priorities is captured by Pastor Joe Boyd who says, "I read the gospels over and over and nothing I was doing on Sunday morning was what I thought Jesus would be doing if he were here."[22] This orientation toward the Jesus of the Gospels and the early church means that these new models of ministry focus on mission by trying to take Jesus' acceptance of, and interaction with, "sinners" and outcasts seriously. It also means that they try to take Jesus' anti-religious establishment message seri-

---

22. Gibbs and Bolger, *Emerging Churches*, 47.

ously by rejecting traditional approaches to ministry and experimenting with new approaches as well as embracing a more eclectic spirituality and theology. While questions about Paul's over-influence on Christianity and the emerging churches' ability to translate Jesus' message properly can be debated, what is clear is that these new models are deeply committed to trying to capture the essence of early Christian belief and practice. This orientation can be helpful to the Christian movement in general as it calls the church back to a reconsideration of its central person and core message.

An Attempt to Engage a Postmodern, Post-Christian Culture

New models of ministry are almost exclusively "missional" in their orientation. This means that they understand the need for the church to be outward focused and connected to the community that it finds itself in. Furthermore, it means adopting the perspective that the church needs to understand itself as a missionary to the culture in which it is situated. Traditional missionaries who go to foreign countries have to learn to speak the language, understand the new culture, and relate to the people that they live among in order to contextualize the Christian message. New models of missional ministry perceive the role of the church in postmodern, post-Christian society in a similar way.

Scot McKnight, using the categories of Doug Pagitt, identifies the way that these new models engage culturally by how they approach postmodernism as a philosophy. Some people minister *to* postmoderns, some minister *with* postmoderns, and some minister *as* postmoderns. The first group see postmodern people as trapped by an evil philosophy from which they need to be saved, the second see postmodernism as the reality of their context and thus accept the fact that Christians must figure out how to minister within that context, and those in the third choose to minister as postmoderns, embracing the key tenants of postmodernism and identifying themselves with it.[23] Most new-model churches fall into the second or third group and embrace the realities of postmodernism in their ministries.

---

23. McKnight, "Five Streams."

An Attempt to Embody and Proclaim a Holistic Gospel

New models of ministry often place emphasis on the function and practice of the gospel in public life. They are committed to proclaiming a gospel that goes beyond the offer of spiritual salvation to a gospel that can impact every aspect of human life and affect local communities for the better. This reflects their commitment to practice over belief. McKnight has observed that praxis—how the faith is lived out—is the primary characteristic of emerging models of the church.[24] This means that their ministry is oriented toward doing works of service in their communities that will bring tangible benefits, being supportive of initiatives designed to help the poor and disenfranchised, and standing up against injustice in its various forms locally, nationally, and internationally. These activities are considered just as much proclaiming the gospel as is verbal witness; in some ways they are even more powerful as they embody Kingdom values and bring them to bear on daily life. This emphasis also helps to awaken the church as a whole to the need for a balanced ministry that does not neglect the needs of the poor and/or the non-verbal proclamation of the gospel. Instead of focusing solely on the goal of saving souls for heaven, the church also needs to proclaim a holistic vision for everyday life.

POTENTIAL CRITICISMS OF NEW CHURCH MODELS

When significant change is being recommended to any institution or movement there is inevitably push back or cautions to pay attention to as well. When those recommended changes begin to be implemented, as they are in emerging congregations all across Canada and other parts of the Western world, the reaction can become even more intense as established patterns of believing and doing are explicitly critiqued by these new initiatives. Some cautions have been offered to these new movements. Whether these critiques have merit or not a few of them need to be noted here.[25]

---

24. Ibid.

25. A couple of books that provide a critique of many of the developments offered in this chapter are Carson, *Becoming Conversant with the Emerging Church*; Davidson and Milbank, *For the Parish*.

Just a Reaction against Establishment Christianity

Emerging models of church ministry may be characterized as primarily a movement of protest in which participants are reacting against their conservative heritage. Particularly in its early manifestations, emergent books and blogs were more preoccupied with this protest than with any genuinely constructive agenda. In other words, there is an argument to be made that these emerging movements frequently fail to live up to their own rhetoric regarding their ideals. Furthermore, the characterization of the "traditional" church presented by many who are advocating for new models can sometimes be a gross caricature that resembles only a certain segment of the established church. It is not completely fair to say that the established church is unconcerned and uninvolved in benevolence and sincere Christian living. If proper attention is not paid to core doctrines of orthodox Christian faith the emerging church movement's accommodation to postmodernism could have the same practical effects as liberal Christianity's accommodation of modernism did (which led to the decline of the movement).

Theologically Suspect and in Places Even Heretical

The emerging models that enthusiastically embrace postmodernism and reject epistemological foundationalism and who willingly enter into the deconstruction of biblical texts and the employment of a more narrative approach to hermeneutics may end up tolerating a range of doctrinal and moral positions in areas that have traditionally been considered non-negotiable in traditional Christian settings. The views held by some in emerging Christian circles may lead to untraditional views on doctrines such as substitutionary atonement, salvation by faith, the nature and/or existence of hell, the sovereignty of God, and homosexuality. Will these emerging movements continue to move in directions that are clear departures from traditional Christian beliefs and practices? This remains an open question.

Overly Focused on the Social Gospel

Some proponents of emerging models have a view of God's Kingdom that is narrowly focused on improving social conditions while ignoring eternal matters. Mainline churches embraced the social gospel in the mid-twentieth century in order to respond to the ills of society and to keep themselves relevant as a cultural movement. However, some would argue that this choice made them even less relevant to society because the church was unable to deliver social services as well as the government. In the process of losing some of their former theological convictions the mainline churches have continued to suffer ongoing decline and irrelevance in the minds of many. Could a similar emphasis on social improvement at the expense of a call to personal salvation lead to a duplication of the same fate for emerging Christianity in the future?

Conclusion: What Does This Mean for Global Christianity?

How does all of this fit into the changing nature of global Christianity? Do these new models of ministry have a relationship to the larger, global trends that are developing in the global Christian movement? Some concluding reflections on these questions may help to put these new trends into a larger perspective.

Emerging Christianity in Canada Tends to Direct Mission Locally

While churches employing new models are often explicitly concerned about being "missional," most of their missional energy is directed to local initiatives, though many emerging congregations also have a vision for overseas projects. In its attempt to address an increasingly unchurched local population, the emerging church has taken on a missional focus that predominantly looks to its immediate surroundings. Whether it is a new model of congregational gathering, or a group that establishes itself in a poor neighborhood, these churches are focused on reaching the community in which they are planted. This is understandable, especially when the church is experiencing decline and the need for mission seems to be so great. The long term effect of this shift on new models of ministry that are local in focus instead of on foreign missions is yet to be seen; more in-depth research on this phenomenon is needed. The movement may result in a diminished vision for global mission in every segment of the church.

Can the New Christendom Help Us?

The decline of Christianity in a country like Canada and the ensuing shift of missional focus begs the question: "Will the emergence of a robust church in South America, China, and Africa have an impact on the church in Canada?" More to the point: "Can missionaries from South America, China, or Africa help the church in Canada to reach Canadians?" These questions point to a further question, "Can the missional movement of the past 150 years be geographically reversed?"[26] These are provocative questions. Should the emerging church in Canada be preparing for this reversal and working on ways to facilitate it? In many ways the more informal, communal, and spirit-infused Christianity that is growing in other parts of the world is not unlike the Christianity that the emerging church is looking for. The Christianity of the "New Christendom" is in many ways defined by simplicity, communal relationships, and signs and wonders. Perhaps the church that has traditionally received missionaries from nations like Canada can become the church that now comes to the aid of its former benefactor. This provokes the further question, "Would the church in Canada be glad to receive such help?" The answer to this question remains unclear at this time.[27]

New Models Are an Inevitable Post-Christendom Phenomenon

In ancient times Israel was forced into exile by the expansionist policies of Babylonia and as a result they experienced the reality of being "post:" post-land, post-king, post-temple. This loss of national autonomy and being forced to the margins of a new society was an experience that is not unlike the loss of "Christendom" that the church in Canada is facing. This experience ultimately called Israel to find new ways of understanding and practicing their faith. Exile reconstituted Israel's identity around issues like God's presence in a foreign land, their call as a nation to holiness, and their identity as a light to the Gentiles (mission). This reconsideration

---

26. In many ways this is already underway as South Korea has become a significant sender of missionaries to various parts of the world, as have some Latin American and African countries.

27. Phillip Jenkins has noted that immigrant churches are playing a unique role in strengthening the church in Europe as well as contributing to evangelism on that continent. See Jenkins, *God's Continent*. This reality is observable in Canada and the USA as well.

and reconfiguration of the faith was an inevitable response to drastically changed circumstances. It was ultimately valuable for Israel.

The decline of Western Christendom is part of the story of global Christianity and it is forcing the church in Canada, as it is in other places, to refocus on questions of identity. Just as it was in ancient Israel, this is an inevitable response to deep cultural change. The way that the Canadian church negotiates these changes may facilitate its survival and even its renewal. Its journey may even prove informative for churches in other post-Christian societies.

Bibliography

Adeney, Francis S. *Graceful Evangelism: Christian Witness in a Complex World.* Grand Rapids: Baker, 2010.
Arpin-Ricci, Jamie. *The Cost of Community: Jesus, St. Francis and Life in the Kingdom.* Downers Grove, IL: InterVarsity, 2011.
Bessenecker, Scott. *The New Friars: The Emerging Movement Serving the World's Poor.* Downers Grove, IL: InterVarsity, 2006.
Bibby, Reginald Wayne. *Beyond the Gods and Back: Religion's Demise and Rise and Why It Matters.* Lethbridge, AB: Project Canada Books, 2011.
———. *The Emerging Millennials: How Canada's Newest Generation Is Responding to Change and Choice.* Lethbridge, AB: Project Canada Books, 2009.
Campbell, Heidi. "Congregation of the Disembodied: A Look at Religious Community on the Internet." In *Virtual Morality: Morals, Ethics and the New Media*, edited by Mark J. P. Wolf, 179–99. New York: Peter Lang, 2003.
Carson, D.A. *Becoming Conversant with the Emerging Church.* Grand Rapids: Zondervan, 2005.
Claiborne, Shane. *The Irresistible Revolution.* Grand Rapids: Zondervan, 2006.
Davidson, Andrew, and Alison Milbank. *For the Parish: A Critique of Fresh Expressions.* London: SCM, 2010.
Duin, Julia. *Quitting Church: Why the Faithful Are Fleeing and What to Do about It.* Grand Rapids: Baker, 2008.
Estes, Doug. *SimChurch: Being the Church in the Virtual World.* Grand Rapids: Zondervan, 2009.
Frost, Michael. *Exiles: Living Missionally in a Post-Christian Culture.* Peabody, MA: Hendrickson, 2006.
Gibbs, Eddie, and Ryan Bolger. *Emerging Churches: Creating Christian Community in Postmodern Culture.* Grand Rapids: Baker, 2006.
Henderson, Jim, Todd Hunter, and Craig Spinks. *Outsider Interviews: A New Generation Speaks Out on Christianity.* Grand Rapids: Baker, 2010.
Jenkins, Philip. *God's Continent: Christianity, Islam and Europe's Religious Crisis.* New York: Oxford University Press, 2007.

———. *The Next Christendom: The Coming of Global Christianity*. Oxford: Oxford University Press, 2002.
Marshall, David B. *Secularizing the Faith: Canadian Protestant Clergy and the Crisis of Belief, 1850–1940*. Toronto: University of Toronto Press, 1992.
McKnight, Scot. "Five Streams of the Emerging Church." *Christianity Today* 51, no. 2 (2007) 34–39. Online: http://www.christianitytoday.com/ct/2007/february/11.35.html?start=2.
McLaren, Brian. *Generous Orthodoxy: Why I Am a Missional + Evangelical + Post/Protestant + Liberal/Conservative + Mystic/Poetic + Biblical + Charismatic/Contemplative + Fundamentalist/Calvinist + Anabaptist/Anglican + Methodist + Catholic + Green + Incarnational + Depressed-yet-hopeful + Emergent + Unfinished Christian*. Grand Rapids: Zondervan, 2004.
Morganthaler, Sally. "Leadership in a Flattened World: Grassroots Culture and the Demise of the CEO Model." In *An Emergent Manifesto of Hope*, edited by Doug Pagitt and Tony Jones, 175–88. Grand Rapids: Baker, 2007.
Stone, Bryan. *Evangelism after Christendom: The Theology and Practice of Christian Witness*. Grand Rapids: Brazos, 2007.
Studebaker, Steve, and Lee Beach. "Emerging Churches in Post Christian Canada." *Religions* 3, no. 1 (2012) 862–79.
Taylor, Charles. *A Secular Age*. Cambridge, MA: Harvard University Press, 2007.
Thomlinson, Dave. *The Post-Evangelical*. Grand Rapids: Zondervan, 2003.
Zdero, Rad. *Global House Church Movement*. Pasadena: William Carey, 2004.

4

Servants of Christ, Servants of Caesar
A Theology for Life in Post-Christian America

Steven M. Studebaker

Fretting about the decline of Western Christianity is common. Proposals proliferate on ways churches can better engage the post-Christian culture.[1] Ryan Bolger's *The Gospel after Christendom* looks at churches from New Zealand to Latin America and addresses pressing issues of our time, from the environmental crisis to immigration and pluralism. It proposes pathways to rejuvenate the Western church, from developing missional identities to holistic and transformational mission. It showcases a set of innovative church ministries, from a Hip-Hop Church to the Jesus Dojo and Urban Abbey. Whether under the banner of emergent churches, New Monastic communities, the missional movement, or something else, these efforts share a common cause to figure out how the church can respond to its new cultural place—a place in an age called post-Christendom. The term "post-Christendom" is a euphemism. It denotes the church's disenfranchisement from mainstream Western culture. It names a place of dislocation and marginalization. Exploring ways to adapt to the reality of post-Christendom is therefore worthwhile.

This fussing about post-Christendom, however, obscures something more profound, especially for American Christians.[2] Sitting in church on

---

1. For example, see Bolger, *Gospel after Christendom*.

2. The argument of this chapter applies more broadly to Western and not only American Christians. I focus on American Christians for the following reasons: (1) This book

Sunday, they may feel like aliens in the wider culture; however, the rest of the week they are quite at home in it. They are embedded in the life of the American Empire. They work, raise families, and consume its media, entertainment, and recreation.

The dawn of post-Christendom confronts Christians with the reality that their culture is not Christian. Cultural dislocation makes it harder for American Christians to relate their life in the world to the kingdom of God. During the era of Christendom, with the assumption that the culture was Christian, everything one did was ostensibly service to God's kingdom. After all, when you promoted the spread of the American nation, you participated in extending a Christian culture. When missionaries taught Indians white ways on the American frontier, they saw this as making them Christians. Teaching them to farm and wear European-style clothing differed little from teaching them Christian doctrines.

One consequence of post-Christendom is that many Christians effectively live in two worlds. One is the Christian bubble: in this world, they pray, attend church, sing worship songs, and take part in various church activities. Connecting this world with the kingdom of God is fairly easy—not so for the rest of their lives. The second world includes work, recreation, education, and leisure activities. How this stuff relates to the Christian life is anyone's guess. Western Christians tend to divide life into two domains, one secular and one spiritual. They need a better worldview, one that integrates these different areas of life. Before turning to that task, however, this essay describes four popular responses to post-Christendom among Evangelicals and the problem of what I call Humpty Dumpty theology.[3]

---

treats implications of globalization for particular contexts of Christianity. (2) Although the West, with America its principal state, shares a common culture, it also has diversity. France and America are both Western, but clearly they are not homogenous. (3) Finally, the cultural context for American Christians is distinct from that of Christians in other Western states. Their national identity is different and so is their experience of post-Christendom from that of their counterparts in other Western nations. Notwithstanding these differences, from the broader perspective of relative global civilizations, Western Christians have more cultural affinities than disparities.

3. Lee Beach's chapter also discusses post-Christendom. It focuses on ways Canadian churches adapt to the new cultural context. My chapter recognizes that post-Christendom is the cultural reality for North American Christians. My concern, however, is to reflect on Christian identity and participation in North American culture rather than ways the church can adapt its ministry styles to a post-Christian culture.

The Globalization of Christianity

Crusade or the Ghetto?

The church has responded to its cultural marginalization in two basic ways: going on crusade or going to the ghetto. Crusading conflates church and culture. It assumes the legitimacy of Christendom. Its proponents believe that America and Canada are essentially Christian nations—or at least they were. Though the forces of secularism have gained ground, the war is not lost. Christians must rally, sally forth, and take back the culture for God. Crusading wants a *reconquista* for Christendom. This view confuses Christian participation in culture with Christianizing culture. This chapter will focus on the second form—ghetto Christianity.

Margins Christianity

Ghetto Christianity has three forms. The first moves to the margins. These Christians not only accept the reality of post-Christendom, they reject the Christendom project altogether. The church was never meant to be a social power broker, they say. Jesus was poor. He came to the world not in Caesar's palace, but in a backwater village; he ministered to people in the gutter of the Empire. Christians today should do the same, forsake upper-middle-class privilege and the comfort of the suburbs and move to the city. They should live with, or at least near, the poor and destitute. The church should subvert, not collaborate with, the dominant culture. The patron saints of this movement are Anabaptist theologians John Howard Yoder and Stanley Hauerwas and Christian activist Shane Claiborne. This form of evangelical Christianity appeals to many young people since they find it a place for an adventurous life of faith. For lack of a better term, emerging churches fall into this category. Many of them engage culture in creative ways and commit significant resources to social justice ministries, yet many of them (though not all) reflect the "margins" mentality. Their activism tends to be local and not directed to the broader issues in society—for example, what policies Christians should support in respect to unfunded liability reform.[4]

---

4. The principal drivers of America's long-term insolvency are the unfunded entitlement programs of Social Security, Medicare, and Medicaid, the last two being the prime movers. The problem is the gap between the government's promised benefits to entitlement recipients and the government's projected tax revenues that fund these programs. For a gloomy projection on the future debt obligation of these programs, see Kotlikoff and Burns, *Clash of Generations*, 30–31.

Fortress Christianity

The second form of ghetto Christianity defends the battlements of Fortress Ecclesia. The culture is lost, overrun by heathen hordes; the beleaguered church must defend the ramparts of orthodoxy. These churches gravitate toward conservative forms of Christianity. Figures such as John Piper and Don Carson and organizations such as the Gospel Coalition are examples. Fear catalyzes these churches. They fear the further erosion of the church; they fear the disappearance of the cultural world that shared their values and lifestyle. They become shrill. Truth must be defended, accommodation shunned. The voice of the church narrows. A handful of issues—such as gay marriage and abortion—transcribe the circumference of its moral imagination. A short list of doctrines—biblical inerrancy and penal substitutionary atonement—defines the true faith. Waver from these and forfeit your soul. The church is the citadel of Christ and the world outside is a godless wasteland, a place where evil minions lurk to waylay the Christian faithful. This strident and defensive form of Christianity offers solace to many weary sojourners. It offers the soothing narcotic of easy alternatives: unflinching fealty to traditional beliefs and practices or the infidelity of churches that have lost their first love.

Club Christianity

Club Christianity is the final and probably the most popular option. It is the urbane Christianity of middle- and upper-middle-class evangelical churches. Implicitly at peace with secularization, it opts neither to go on crusade to take back the culture for God, nor to lapse into latter-day fundamentalism. Secularization assumes that modern societies marginalize religion. The conveniences of modern life and state assistance programs displace the social need for God and the church. People once trusted God and the church for their security and support, but now they put their faith in technology, medicine, and the beneficence of the bureaucratic state. Religion has no relevance for public life; the private spiritual life is the only realm left for it. Mainstream evangelical Christianity serves this religious niche by fashioning Christianity into a religious product of personal piety. It provides therapies for the soul. It champions Christianity for the individual spiritual life. It is the church of Rick Warren, Bill Hybels, and mega-church Christianity. Club Christianity is not anti-cultural like the first two types of ghetto Christianity. On the contrary, it embraces the culture's values of success and efficiency.[5] Its spirituality is sequestered, but not its participation in the world.

These three views misconstrue the Christian's relation to the world, the state, and culture. They are either too separatist or too binary. They reject mainstream culture as the proper place of Christian activity. Club Christianity is content to service the cloister of personal spirituality. "Move to the margins" and "run to the ramparts" mentalities are Manichean. According to them, the world is evil; Christians are part of the church and the coming kingdom of God. The two realms are antithetical to one another. The state is satanic and therefore Christians must either subvert it through social justice ministry or check its attacks on the citadel of Christ. The common problem with these three views is Humpty Dumpty theology.

HUMPTY DUMPTY THEOLOGY

Some traditional Christian theology fragments life. It breaks the Christian life into secular and sacred pieces that can never be put together again—the kingdom of this world and the kingdom of God. This is Humpty Dumpty theology. Two ways for understanding the relationship between these two worlds are popular. One is the image of the earthly and heavenly cities. The other is the theology of common and special grace. Augustine's "two cities" is a good place to start.[6]

Babylon and Jerusalem

Augustine lived during the decay of the western half of the Roman Empire. The Vandal Kingdom was moving steadily east across North Africa. Hippo, Augustine's home city, fell soon after his death. Some blamed the fall on the Christian religion, but Augustine argued that this view confused the

---

5. Chu, "Willow Creek."

6. Overall my assessment of Luther's two kingdom's theology is similar to what follows on Augustine. Although granting that vocations in this world are good in so far as they contribute to the order of this world, it subordinates them to the spiritual kingdom (e.g., spiritual over physical, gospel over reason). It assumes discontinuity between not only the way of the world (i.e., Babylon) and the kingdom of God, but also the embodied, physical world, and heaven and the spiritual kingdom that ultimately supplant it. Thus, Luther's two kingdoms theology is too hierarchical and dualistic. For Luther's two kingdoms theology, see Wright, *Luther's Understanding of God's Two Kingdoms*.

Empire with the kingdom of God. Rome may have embraced Christianity; nevertheless, Rome was a manifestation of what Augustine called the earthly city. Rome is Babylon. The church, on the other hand, co-exists with the earthly city but belongs to the heavenly one, the City of God. Orientation is the key difference between the two cities: the devotion of the one is toward God and love but the devotion of the other is toward the things of this world and power. The earthly city is not equivalent to any one nation, state, or empire; it refers more to the way of the world than to a particular city.[7] In fact, all cities, nations, and civilizations express the earthly city, and Revelation's Lake of Fire is their destination. The heavenly city will not be completed until the establishment of the everlasting kingdom.

The image of the two cities showcases the differences between the cities but obscures the similarities between them. The earthly city goes to hell; the heavenly one becomes the New Jerusalem. The first city has its heart set on the things of this world but the second loves God and seeks shalom. However, the activity that goes on in them is in many respects the same. They are places of commerce, politics, education, and the arts. The differences are profound, yet so are the continuities. How should Christians understand this continuity between participation in the earthly and heavenly cities?

Christian theology often assumes that the church and spiritual matters and the rest of human life are of different orders. Even the Reformed tradition, noted for its attention to the cultural mandate, carries this ambivalence. Cultural work is the arena of common grace whereas church, God, and salvation form the realm of special grace; the two spheres are distinct orders of grace. Common grace is important. God calls Christians to serve in the institutions of the world, contribute to the arts, and serve civic society. Common grace, however, is not part of the order of saving grace. Saving grace saves the soul. It relates to the Christian life, the world of the church. Ambivalence toward the world is the inevitable result. Work in the world may be valuable, but ultimately ranks beneath work in the church.

These orders of grace provide the template for the way many Christians think about their life in Babylon. For them, God has different providential agendas for the heavenly kingdom and the one of this world. While waiting for the advent of the New Jerusalem, Christians should find their identity in the church and not the world. Christians can get a glimpse of

---

7. Augustine, *City of God*, 18.54 (*NPNF* 2:395–96), 19.10 (*NPNF* 2:406), 19.17 (*NPNF* 2:412–13). More generally, see books 15–22.

God's kingdom in church, but the world, the surrounding culture, is a secular place. Babylon may not be entirely bad, but it is not God's kingdom.

A comment from a former colleague illustrates this perspective. "We are fortunate compared to your wife. Everything we do with our jobs relates to the kingdom. Your wife has to carve out time on Sunday and maybe a mid-week service to serve the kingdom." My colleague and I were both professors in the ministry department of a Christian institution of higher education. My wife, however, is one of those bottom feeding corporate bankers. She works with filthy lucre. She spends her day in the belly of the beast. Obviously her work in corporate finance has zero to do with the sanctified Christian life; indeed, she requires daily absolution and purification. My colleague's point was that as professors in a Christian institution the entirety of our professional lives—our teaching, mentoring, preaching—relates to God's kingdom. We serve the kingdom Monday through Friday and Sunday too. However, we take off most Saturdays because, after all, even God took a Sabbath rest. Most people like my wife are not so fortunate. They have "secular" jobs. The greater share of their lives deals with temporal and earthly things, not the eternal and heavenly matters of God's kingdom. They are lucky to serve the kingdom from 7:00 to 8:30 Wednesday evening and 10:00 to 11:30 Sunday morning. They will squeak into the kingdom, but the bejeweled crowns will go to people like us. Common among evangelical Christians, this viewpoint is nonetheless unfortunate and unbiblical.

Common and Special Grace

The doctrines of common and special grace divide human activity into secular and spiritual territories. Life in the world—commerce, youth sports, leisure, and the arts—is the realm of common grace. Common grace restrains sin, provides human beings with a moral sense that keeps societies more or less civil, and funds cultural production. Common grace is God's work in the lives of people unrelated to their salvation. Special or saving grace is the unique operation of God that inspires faith and empowers the Christian life.[8] Common grace and special grace, although not opposed, are discrete divine programs.[9] The key difference is that common grace has

---

8. Erickson, *Christian Theology*, 153–54; Demarest, *General Revelation*, 13–14, 228, 233, 250.

9. For example, even though Terrance L. Tiessen sees both common and special grace

nothing to do with the order of special grace. A person can participate fully in common grace, but never touch special grace. In other words, common grace does not save the soul—only special grace does that.[10] This distinction is precisely the problem.[11]

It is problematic because it renders life in the world inconsequential. According to this view, Christians should devote their energies to spiritual disciplines, personal piety, and church ministries. The earth and human activities related to it fall within the realm of common grace. They distract Christians from more important spiritual matters; therefore, they must be subordinated to the latter. Work in the world may be valuable, but it is beneath work in the church. Evangelism and prayer, for example, are activities of special grace, whereas building a business and becoming a better grade school teacher are lesser activities of common grace. Evangelism and prayer have eternal value, but business and education will pass away with this world. Wise Christians give their energies to things of eternal consequence and not those of this ephemeral world. They agree with C. T. Studd's sentiment, "Only one life, 'twill soon be past; only what's done for Christ will last." Cultivating culture is not the concern of special grace, Christian ministry, and the kingdom of God. The affairs of creation and human civilization are not the place for the saving work of Christ; they are not the place where Christians seek to "work out [their] salvation with fear and trembling" (Phil 2:12).

---

as benefits of Christ's atoning work, he still maintains that common grace is non-salvific. See Tiessen, *Who Can Be Saved*, 100–101, 396–400, 416, 418, 422–23.

10. Demarest, *General Revelation*, 247–53; Erickson, *Christian Theology*, 153–54; Grudem, *Systematic Theology*, 658, 658–63. For Pentecostals endorsing this view, see Higgins, "God's Inspired Word," 75–76; Menzies and Horton, *Bible Doctrines*, 20–21.

11. The Dutch Reformed tradition does this very well. A key figure in this tradition is Abraham Kuyper. The distinction between common and special grace arises from a Reformed view of election. God gives common grace to all people, but only special grace, the grace of regenerated life, to the elect. So, though Kuyper has a robust theology of common grace that fosters the purposes of the created order (e.g., human cultural production and social organization), it remains distinct from the grace of salvation. For an introduction to Kuyper's theology of common grace and its relationship to Christian participation in society, see Bacote, *Spirit in Public Theology*, esp. 96–107. For Kuyper's understanding of the relationship between the Holy Spirit and the orders of common and special grace, see Kuyper, *Work of the Holy Spirit*, 45–46, 288–91, 295, 310–13.

THE GLOBALIZATION OF CHRISTIANITY

PUTTING HUMPTY TOGETHER AGAIN

The problem with this is that the categories of common and special grace tear apart Scripture's unified vision of redemption. God does not have two providential orders, a secular and a spiritual one. God wants to bring all creation to its proper way of participating in the divine life (Rom 8:20–21). Creation and redemption are distinct in the sense that God redeems creation, but not in their providential program and end. God has one goal—the redemption of creation. Creation and redemption are not two separate orders, spheres, or modalities of divine activity, but one program in which God redeems creation.[12]

This unity of creation and redemption does not deny a conceptual distinction between them. It sets aside, however, a dichotomy that divides them into separate divine programs. God does not have earthly and heavenly agendas. Jesus prayed for God's kingdom to come on earth (Matt 6:10). For example, at the moment that God creates human life, God does so for no other purpose than to nurture in people loving patterns of life with creation, other human persons, and the triune Godhead. Moreover, whatever people do in and through their lives either contributes to or detracts from achieving God's creative purpose for their lives. Conceptually, a distinction can be drawn between God's act of creating a human person and the purpose for that creation. The distinction, however, is more logical and abstract than descriptive of disparate divine programs.

The problem is not with distinctions. The activity of politics differs from that of the biotechnology research facility. Worshipping God in song and going fly-fishing are not the same. The problem is the assumption that creation and redemption are two things, and that God's plan of redemption does not include creation. Christian thinking about salvation typically focuses on heaven. Christians believe that heaven is not on earth; wherever it is, it is not here. Furthermore, it is different than life here. It is spiritual, not physical. Work, recreation, and the arts are earthly, not heavenly. They are part of creation, and though permissible for the Christian, they are not part of the Christian life as such. A comment made in a sermon expresses this theology: "It's okay to go bass fishing, but make sure you take a friend to witness to." Witnessing is spiritual and, therefore, a worthy Christian endeavor, but bass fishing by itself is in Christian Never Never Land. This

---

12. McFague, *Body of God*, 179–82. McFague makes a case for creation as the place of salvation using the metaphor of the universe as the body of God.

theology is not biblical; in fact, God's future kingdom bears little resemblance to the popular Christian notion of salvation and heaven.

Recognizing that God's redemptive work takes in all of creation and all human endeavor grounds the Christian's relation to the state. It means that life in this world bears continuity with life in the everlasting kingdom. The basic patterns and activities of life in Babylon and the New Jerusalem are more similar than different. The book of Revelation portrays the New Jerusalem flying down from the sky to the earth. The kingdom has a city and also a restored environment. The New Earth of Revelation 22 looks like Eden. The "river of the water of life" flows through its main street and trees perpetually bear fruit along its banks. A city, a river, trees, not to mention the New Heaven and the New Earth—these are creation. The parched land, the thorns and thistles of the world outside of Eden are gone. The New Earth is a lush landscape, but it is creation, not a celestial place called "heaven." The New Jerusalem is a sanctified city, but a city it is.

CITIZEN SOJOURNERS

The Bible gives Christians two bearings for living in this world. The first encourages Christians to cultivate life in this world. Thus, they are citizens of Babylon. The second warns that the world is not their home. They are therefore sojourners in Babylon. Here are two paradoxical truths: you must settle and put down roots, and you are a foreigner in a strange land. How can Christians be both sojourners and settlers? Surely they must be one or the other? No. The relationship between the Christian, culture, the state, and the coming kingdom of God is complex. The desire for simple slogans is understandable. Sound bite Christianity soothes the soul; it does not, however, nurture a mature one. The Bible is practical, not simplistic, because life is complicated. The Bible provides two bearings for navigating life in this world. Paul and John represent these two orientations, and although they seem opposed, their theologies are compatible. Taken together they clarify a complex situation: Christians are citizen sojourners in Babylon. The guidance given by Paul and John, moreover, is both theological and practical. However, before we examine their advice, the difference between American Christians and their first-century counterparts needs attention.

The Globalization of Christianity

Christian and American

American Christians are citizens of Babylon, but the same could not be said of the early Christians. They were an illegal sect that underwent periodic persecution. Most came from the under classes, although later the movement drew from a range of social levels. The majority of first-century Christians, however, lived on the margins of Roman society. Jesus came from a small town on the eastern edge of the Roman Empire and the disciples came from the underbelly of the Empire. They were outcasts from mainstream society. They lived in the Roman Empire, but were not of the Empire.[13]

American Christians are different. They are of the American Empire. They are its doctors, professors, politicians, business people, skilled workers, nurses, and more. They are not, for the most part, on the margins of empire. Even missional Christians who live in dystopian urbanscapes, often as part of new monastic communities, do so by choice. Most can return to the more comfortable suburbs at will. They are part of the mainstream imperial order. Rather than being persecuted, their religion is tolerated. Though certain elements of the culture ridicule it, most American Christians suffer no negative consequences for their Christian faith, and many may actually benefit from it. American Christians are citizens of both Babylon and the New Jerusalem. They are the technocrats and bureaucrats of Babylon but they are also saints of God's kingdom. They are servants of both Christ and Caesar. How should they understand these two identities?

Citizens and Sojourners

The Apostles Paul and John provide two biblical bearings that connect life in Babylon with that in the New Jerusalem. Paul calls Christians to be good citizens of the Empire. Paul's advice is the New Testament version of Jeremiah's guidance to "seek the peace and prosperity of the city" (Jer 29:8). John, however, warns that this world is enemy territory. The Beast of Babylon will harry Christian saints until Jesus comes. How do we reconcile Paul's theology of obeying the authorities because God appoints them with John's "it's the end of the world as we know it" battle in Revelation?

---

13. By the second century, however, Christians participated in a much broader spectrum of Roman life. For instance, by the 170s Christians were soldiers in the army.

For Paul, civilization and government organize human life.[14] They please God and they can facilitate human flourishing in a way that atomized life cannot. The everlasting kingdom is a heavenly civilization. The New Jerusalem does not repudiate culture and society; it redeems them. Paul's advice expresses this idea. He is not ignorant of Rome's seedy underbelly, but in his context, what is the alternative to participating with Rome? Anarchy or the nomadic and tribal cultures beyond the boundaries of the Empire hardly seem preferable. For all its injustices, life within is probably preferable to life outside the Empire. From the third through fifth centuries Eurasian peoples migrated into and along the borders of Rome because they believed their lives would be better off if they did so. Rome was brutal, and at times murderous, exploitive, and oppressive. However, it was also prosperous. It had developed road and trade networks; it had laws and a sophisticated bureaucracy. Within the Empire, a person could travel with a fair degree of safety on all-weather roads from Antioch all the way to London.

God is not anti-state, anti-empire, or anti-civilization. God does not call Christians to withdraw to the margins of society. Paul spoke to people on the periphery, but he did not call them there. He does not make social disenfranchisement an ideal. As far as possible, Christians should participate in society, according to Paul. They should be citizens of the Empire.

Today "empire" is bad word. Empires oppress. They exploit the weak for the benefit of the political and financial elites. They impose cultural homogeneity, they demand absolute obeisance, they do nasty things, and they run amock. All of this is true. Yet, they also are places where families thrive, students receive education, and careers flourish. They make possible the development of medical and information technologies that improve human lives. Civilizations and empires are not all bad all the time. Where would you rather live, Stone Age Europe or modern London? Even the poor in a modern Western society are affluent compared to the majority of their pre-modern ancestors. Obesity, once the luxury of the privileged elite, is now a plague on the poorest.

Paul sees the state, or at least the system of government, as God-given. It organizes society. This domain of human activity is neither God-forsaken nor outside the redemptive program. History culminates in the

---

14. Paul reflects a dominant tradition of Jewish thought found in prophetic and wisdom literature of the Old Testament. See Dunn, *Romans 9–16*, 761–62, 764, 770–72; Moo, *Romans*, 798–99.

New Jerusalem. The City of God replaces Babylon, just as the resurrected body supersedes the mortal one. Final redemption neither impugns the current body and state nor renders them bereft of God's grace. Paul has a positive theology of culture.

Paul's theology inspires two practices: discern the patterns that are consistent with God's kingdom and adapt to them, but subvert and transform the Empire where it is at odds with God's kingdom. Christians can pay taxes and participate in the economic life of the Empire. Paul's advice arises from his theology of culture. The state, the system of government, can be a source of good. The system is not fundamentally immoral; it has a divine purpose. Civilization, culture, and government organize human activity. This theology suggests that Christians should inhabit culture. They should take part in it, though without debasing their faith.

The particular political system shapes the way Christians pursue these two practices. Christians in America, for example, have the ability to influence public policy in ways inconceivable to Paul or to many Christians living today under repressive regimes. Paul's advice to Philemon and Onesimus may look passive to American Christians. Christians in a modern democratic state, however, have more avenues to access and participate in the political process than their first-century counterparts. Christians in America today can play a direct part in politics; in fact, sitting on the margins is irresponsible. Paul did what he could, given his circumstances; American Christians should, too.

Paul was, however, hard-nosed on certain things. He brooked no compromise with the Galatians who taught both Christ *and* circumcision. Almost everyone is a rigid idealist at some point; discerning where the threshold lies between practical adaptation and perfidious accommodation is the difficulty. Christians can adapt to and participate in many activities of culture, but not all of them. Paul's advice to Philemon is instructive on both scores. Paul called Philemon to transcend the inhumanity of Roman slavery. He was to treat his slave, Onesimus, as a brother in the Lord, treating him according to the grace of God's kingdom. He was also to operate within the system of Rome, however. Onesimus likely remained a slave. For idealists, Paul's counsel was a sell-out to the powers that be. They believe that Paul should have subverted the injustice of the Empire. He should have denounced the shameful institution of slavery. If that meant suffering for Paul or, in the case of Philemon, poverty due to the loss of low-cost laborers, then so be it. Better to be on the side of the angels and dead or poor than with the demons and affluent. That, however, is not Paul's theology. Babylon is not the kingdom of God; nevertheless, its systems and structures are not, for the most part, intrinsically evil.

Paul's way of relating to culture can be applied to the contemporary phenomenon of consumerism. Consumerism is a dominant American myth that holds that the acquisition of ever more things defines personal worth. The measure of human dignity is postal code, make of car, net worth, and career. Admittedly, buying stuff is indispensable for life since few people can produce everything they need to live in a modern society. Specialization of work promotes prosperity; certain people excel at farming, others at finance. A culture that enables people to hone their skills, monetize the fruit of their labor, and then trade for the other necessities and wants of life is efficient. It fosters widespread affluence. Christians, however, should not accede to the cult of consumerism. Human dignity arises from being created in the image of God and being loved by the same God. Discovering and developing personal talent and being productive with it are essential to embodying this image. Reducing life to the accumulation of things is not (Luke 12:15). Christians should abstain from the Kool-Aid of consumerism, yet they should also recognize that, within the scope of human history, America's industrial and consumer society is a place of unparalleled opportunity, freedom, and prosperity.

John, on the other hand, describes a less rosy reality. The state is Babylon and this world is enemy territory. The Beast of Babylon will harry Christian sojourners until Jesus returns. Christians, therefore, should look forward to the New Jerusalem, the kingdom of Christ. They do not hope for the end of empire as such; they long for God's City to supplant the sinful city. The expectation is that one day the New Jerusalem will come. Meanwhile, Christians should not get their hopes up about life in Babylon. This side of the everlasting kingdom, human society will not embody God's grace. In fact, it will often oppose it. The Christendom project failed to recognize this fact, as do current efforts for a Christian *reconquista* of society. The attempt to shape culture was not the problem; thinking that Babylon could be baptized was.

John's advice reflects his theology. Christians should expect their culture to resist, not conciliate them. The world will hate and persecute Christians (John 15:18—16:4). This side of God's kingdom, all civilizations, cultures, states, and empires are Babylon. They are hostile to the kingdom of Christ; they are not the City of God and never will be.

At the same time and along with Paul, John affirms civilization. John's theology is not anti-culture. He is not against life in this world. The funeral pyre of Babylon is not the end of salvation history; the coming of the New Jerusalem is. The everlasting kingdom is not an escape from life in the city. The New Jerusalem does not repudiate the desires that drive civilizations—it fulfills them. God redeems creation. The culmination of redemption is the New Heaven and the New Earth. The everlasting kingdom is a civilization, so it is not entirely different from Babylon in this respect. Its orientation makes it different—it is the civilization of Christ. There, God will dwell with his people; there, people will love God and each other; there, life will be fruitful and unmarred with avarice and indolence.

These two biblical orientations describe the tension of the Christian life. Human beings were made to thrive in this world. God did not create humans for heaven, but made them for life on earth. Eden is the natural human habitat, but they don't live there. They live East of Eden in the land stained by Abel's blood. Made for this world, they have become unnatural to it. God's kingdom is not of this world, the world outside the Garden. However, Eden was not another place; Eden was not extra-terrestrial. It was another way of living in this world. Babylon is the way of the world now. It is a world of darkness, disease, and death. A day is coming, however, when God will restore the more ancient order and the City of God will come. The foundation stones of the New Jerusalem will be laid and its walls will rise. The River of Life will wash away the stain of Abel's blood; it will renew the land. The voice heard by John declared:

> Now the dwelling of God is with them. They will be his people, and God himself will be with them and be their God. He will wipe every tear from their eyes. There will be no more mourning or crying or pain, for the old order has passed away. (Rev 21:3-4 NIV and 22:20 KJV)

What do Christians do in the meantime? They should cultivate the garden in this world because God has not abandoned the world. The first glimmer of the gospel appears in Genesis 3:15, the "proto-evangelium." Here God promises to smite sin. The parched land will breathe again, life will flourish, and hearts will brim with joy. Despair and futility will melt away. The New Heaven and New Earth, the New Jerusalem, and the liberation of creation from its bondage to decay will stamp "paid" on that promise. God does not ask Christians to forsake the world. They are to till the land, plant vineyards, and build cities, striving toward the New Jerusalem while living in Babylon. Creation will become the New Earth. Babylon will give way to the New Jerusalem. But hold on, the New Jerusalem flies out of the sky; it comes down from God. This is a way of saying that the New Jerusalem, the civilization of Christ, will not arise from the way of life outside the Garden. Jesus said his kingdom is not of this world; it comes from God. It nevertheless comes *to* this world.

Conclusion

The decline of Christianity presents American Christians with a problem. In respect to their faith, American culture feels increasingly alien to them, but in respect to almost every other dimension of their life, they feel deep kinship with it. How should they understand their relationship to American culture? Some want to take back the culture for God, others move to the margins and seek solidarity with the poor, and others dig in and defend the citadel of Christ. Most opt for the personal spirituality of middle- and upper-middle-class churches. All, however, miss recognizing the fundamental connection American Christians have with their culture. The challenge for American Christians is to reconcile their identities as saints in God's kingdom and as citizens of the American Empire. The Bible gives Christians two bearings for negotiating these identities. The first encourages Christians to cultivate life in this world because they are citizens of Babylon. The second warns that the world is not their home, since they are sojourners in Babylon and saints of the New Jerusalem. Christians are citizen sojourners who cultivate the kingdom of Christ through their citizenship in Babylon. The theology of the citizen sojourner connects life in Babylon with that in the New Jerusalem. It recognizes both the difference and the continuity between citizenship in Babylon and in the New Jerusalem.

Bibliography

Bacote, Vincent E. *The Spirit in Public Theology: Appropriating the Legacy of Abraham Kuyper*. Grand Rapids: Baker Academic, 2005.

Bolger, Ryan K., ed. *The Gospel after Christendom: New Voices, New Cultures, New Expressions*. Grand Rapids: Baker Academic, 2012.

Chu, Jeff. "How Willow Creek Is Leading Evangelicals by Learning from the Business World." *Fast Company* (December 6, 2010). No pages. Online: http://www.fastcompany.com/1702221/how-willow-creek-leading-evangelicals-learning-business-world

Demarest, Bruce A. *General Revelation: Historical Views and Contemporary Issues*. Grand Rapids: Zondervan, 1982.

Dunn, James D. G. *Romans 9–16*. Word Biblical Commentary 38B. Dallas: Word, 1988.

Erickson, Millard J. *Christian Theology*. Grand Rapids: Baker, 1985.

Grudem, Wayne A. *Systematic Theology: An Introduction to Biblical Doctrine*. Grand Rapids: Zondervan, 1994.

Higgins, John R. "God's Inspired Word." In *Systematic Theology: A Pentecostal Perspective*, edited by Stanley M. Horton, 61–115. Springfield, MO: Logion, 1994.

Kotlikoff, Laurence, and Scott Burns. *The Clash of Generations: Saving Ourselves, Our Kids, and Our Economy*. Cambridge, MA: MIT Press, 2012.

Kuyper, Abraham. *The Work of the Holy Spirit*. Translated by Henri De Vries. 1900. Reprint, Grand Rapids: Eerdmans, 1946.

McFague, Sallie. *The Body of God: An Ecological Theology*. Minneapolis: Fortress, 1993.

Menzies, William W., and Stanley M. Horton. *Bible Doctrines: A Pentecostal Perspective*. Springfield, MO: Logion, 1993.

Moo, Douglas J. *The Epistle to the Romans*. New International Commentary on the New Testament. Grand Rapids: Eerdmans, 1996.

Tiessen, Terrance L. *Who Can Be Saved? Reassessing Salvation in Christ and World Religions*. Downers Grove, IL: InterVarsity, 2004.

Wright, William J. *Martin Luther's Understanding of God's Two Kingdoms: A Response to the Challenge of Skepticism*. Grand Rapids: Baker Academic, 2010.

5

Cross-Cultural Preaching
Proclaiming a Global Faith

Michael P. Knowles

Introduction: The Problem of Cross-Cultural Preaching

More than any other historian of our day, Philip Jenkins has succeeded in changing our perception of Western, and world, Christianity. As a reflection of the postmodern, and, more specifically, postcolonial temper of our times, we have come to acknowledge in general terms that Eurocentric voices and perspectives are but part of a global conversation characterized by the diversity of its many participants and contributors. As concerns the life of the church, Jenkins has pushed our recognition of this cultural and intellectual relativization even further, in two important senses. First, he has clearly demonstrated that far from setting the agenda for any truly global conversation (as may once have been the case), the interests and theological preoccupations of mainline Western churches are now little more than a minority opinion. The center of gravity for contemporary Christian faith—at least in terms of sheer numbers and voices—has decisively shifted toward the so-called "two-thirds" world: to Africa, Asia, and South America. Second, Jenkins has sought to correct certain distortions of historical perspective that are central to Western Christendom's self-perception. Acknowledgment of our diminished influence at the outset of the third millennium is properly matched by the recognition that it was not until well into the second Christian millennium that the Western church emerged as anything more than a minor player on the world scene. Vibrant Christian communities thrived for centuries far to the south and east of either Rome or Constantinople.[1] These two perceptions lead inexorably in the direction of a third: if extensive and influential Christian constituencies in, for example, North Africa or northern Mesopotamia once flourished only to fade from sight, what is to prevent the same fate from befalling the Westernized expressions of Christian faith that we currently consider normative? Indeed, are we not confronted by the sobering conclusion that this very process is already well underway for most if not all of the churches in which we ourselves currently claim membership?

How, then, might preachers of the Christian gospel respond? What changes of perspective or method are required if we are to preach cross-culturally within the larger context of a globalized church? One well-traveled route has been to apologize for the pernicious errors of Eurocentrism and, correspondingly, to rehabilitate and raise to prominence what we term—sometimes with unacknowledged condescension—"voices from the margin." Preachers seek the counsel of "third world" theologians, read biblical texts from the perspective of those who would otherwise remain unheard, and celebrate diversity wherever it is to be found. Even apart from the theological selectivity that typically governs this process, however, it is in one important sense essentially misguided. Notwithstanding the sympathies of postmodernism that tend in this direction, the voice of another cannot be accorded special authority solely because the speaker in question represents a country or culture that has suffered from Western colonization, cultural domination, or economic exploitation. That injustice requires redress is self-evident. Yet the righting of wrongs is not, for its own sake, the ultimate center of gravity or source of inspiration for Christian faith. Rather, all human perspectives are called into question, all attempts at hearing equally weighed and challenged, all calls for justice governed by a scriptural word whose authority transcends cultural location or moral status alone. In response to the postmodern claim that the voice of suffering deserves to be heard first, surely the suffering of Christ offers a perspective by which to interpret—and, in proper measure, validate—all other human suffering and the cries for recognition to which it gives rise.

Lest the intended point be misconstrued, the relativization of one's own voice and a willingness to hear the voice of the "other" (including the

---

1. As chronicled in particular by Jenkins, *Lost History of Christianity*.

marginalized) are indeed essential to the task of Christian proclamation. As Lesslie Newbigin observes,

> the only way in which the gospel can challenge our culturally conditioned interpretations of it is through the witness of those who read the Bible with minds shaped by other cultures. We have to listen to others. This mutual correction is sometimes unwelcome, but it is necessary and it is fruitful.[2]

Still, the self-perception of the Western church offers an apt illustration of the extent to which the concepts of "centrality" and "marginality" are themselves entirely relative. Jenkins notes, for example:

> What Americans customarily think of as Christianity is, often, a specific manifestation of the faith that operates in the post-Enlightenment West. Ideas that might appear natural to the religion do not seem so elsewhere. For many Christians outside the West, it is not obvious that religion should be an individual or privatized matter; that church and state be separate; that secular values predominate in some spheres of life; or that scriptures be evaluated according to the canons of historical scholarship.[3]

Indeed, Jenkins demonstrates that just as the supposedly normative interests of Western Christendom are, in global perspective, anything but, so also the voices that we might consider "marginal" are sometimes closer to a majority view within the context of world Christianity, or world history.[4]

Moreover, immediate and pressing cultural challenges confront us already within our own borders, insofar as urban churches in particular typically include members of many different national origins. Ethnic minority congregations sometimes struggle to accommodate the quite different needs and expectations of first generation immigrants, on the one hand, and their post-immigration children, on the other. Those of the so-called "1.5 generation" sometimes find themselves in cultural limbo, suspended

---

2. Newbigin, *Gospel in a Pluralist Society*, 196–97. This quotation comes from the conclusion to an extraordinarily sensitive and incisive discussion (the influence of which will be evident throughout the present study) of the dialectical relationship between "gospel" and "culture."

3. Jenkins, *New Faces of Christianity*, 181–82.

4. Jenkins proposes just such an exercise in cross-cultural reading: his incisive suggestions include an invitation to interpret Ruth in company with modern-day refugees and exiles, the book of Revelation from the perspective of Christians persecuted by their own government, or the letter of James from the viewpoint of a materially destitute believer (Jenkins, *New Faces of Christianity*, 182–84).

between their culture of ethnic origin and that of their adopted country, belonging to both yet feeling fully at home in neither. Similarly, in ethnically homogenous congregations the "generation gap" looms large—as battle-scarred survivors of our ongoing "worship wars" would be quick to confirm. Not even within a specific generational cohort can cultural homogeneity be assumed; any high school teacher might easily produce evidence to the contrary. Indeed, such is the prominence in our day of electronically-mediated communication that personal, social, and cultural identity is increasingly being shaped by technological considerations that encroach on territory traditionally measured in terms of ethnicity or national allegiance and, within the church, by denominational membership or confessional tradition. Might not the calamitous "greying" of so many North American and European churches reflect, at least in part, failure to communicate across all such cultural boundaries?

The dual challenges of cultural relativization and cross-cultural communication, both of which are central to the task of Christian preaching, raise difficult questions of normativity. Where, for Christian preachers, does our center of value lie? What is the proper source of authentically "Christian" language? And insofar as language itself is intrinsically cultural, is truly cross-cultural proclamation even possible?

Cross-Cultural Preaching and the Culture of the Cross

Before we can examine the challenges of cross-cultural preaching in particular—by which we mean the challenges of communicating Christian faith between social, cultural, and language groups that do not share the same assumptions, values, worldview, or even the same linguistic tools—we first need to face the problem that preaching presents in principle. The problem lies with the nature of the Christian message itself, if by that we intend a message that focuses on the birth, life, ministry, teaching, death, resurrection, and historical-theological significance of Jesus of Nazareth. For that message is at one and the same time culturally specific, supra-cultural, and counter-cultural. It is culturally specific in that it concerns the activities of a particular individual in the Roman province of Judaea during the early years of the Julio-Augustan dynasty. It is, conversely, supra-cultural in the sense that the Christian message (at least by any historically orthodox account) claims to speak of an eternal God entering into the specificity of human history, human culture, human time and space. At the behest of the One whose word brought creation itself out of chaos, the eternal *Logos* becomes what Augustine of Hippo termed a *Verbum infans*, a "word without a word," a word unable to speak, wordlessly expressing its embrace of the human inability to fully articulate the things of God.[5] Christian preaching is equally supra-cultural in the sense that it claims to bear witness to the ultimate supersession of all human culture and history in the resurrection of this same Jesus, representing the inauguration of a "new creation" (cf. 2 Cor 5:17; Gal 6:15). Third, Christian proclamation is counter-cultural in the sense that it asks us to believe that the Lord of time and space, the Creator of all things, permits himself to be crucified by creatures who refuse to hear the word he brings. Because of his crucifixion, preaching about Christ must acknowledge the failure of human culture, even religious culture, to recognize the word of God, incarnate or otherwise. Furthermore, preaching is in principle counter-cultural in the sense that it bids us not only to speak of such things, but even to place our trust in that same crucified word, in what Paul calls "the message of the cross" (ὁ λόγος . . . τοῦ σταυροῦ, 1 Cor 1:18).

In writing thus to a recently founded congregation, Paul is simply reiterating the terms of the Christian message that he and his companions first preached in Corinth (1 Cor 2:1; 15:1). He reminds them:

> the message of the cross is foolishness to those who are perishing, but to us who are being saved it is the power of God. . . . For since in the wisdom of God the world through its wisdom did not know him, God was pleased through the foolishness of what was preached to save those who believe. Jews demand signs and Greeks look for wisdom, but we preach Christ crucified: a stumbling block to Jews and foolishness to Gentiles (1 Cor 1:18, 21–23).

To understand the Christian gospel in such terms is a matter of taking with utmost seriousness the deathly character of the cross. For if Paul is to be believed, the cross attacks us precisely at the point of our highest religious aspiration: it indicates that at the very pinnacle of religious obedience and pious endeavor lies the unexpected risk of opposing God. This irony is beyond counter-intuitive or counter-cultural: it is deeply shocking and offensive. Yet in support of this assertion we may cite the Apostle Peter, whose response to Jesus' announcement of his own imminent death is, "God forbid it, Lord! This must never happen to you" (Matt 16:22); the

---

5. Regarding this motif in Augustine, see Meconi, "Silence Proceeding," 64–65, 74–75 n. 10.

apostles who are amazed and afraid as they follow Jesus toward Jerusalem (Mark 10:32), then abandon him in his hour of need (Mark 14:27–31, 50); or the zealous firebrand named Saul whose passion for the truth of God leads him to persecute the heretics who follow an apparently false Messiah (Acts 8:1–3). Should these illustrations fail to convince, there is, finally, the precedent of the incarnate *Logos* himself, who chooses not to testify in his own defense, then finally falls silent on the cross.[6] The silence of the cross, which brings into clear focus the universal human rejection—on religious grounds, no less—of God's address to us, reduces all remaining voices to silence, and with them the cultures they each represent.

Without the crucifixion, which represents the failure of every human voice without exception, we are left to fight it out amongst ourselves for linguistic and cultural supremacy—for the supremacy either of our own voices, or of whichever alternative views we esteem most highly. Even when we recognize the error of our own presumption as members of a historically dominant culture, and acknowledge the corrective value of heterogenous or hitherto marginalized voices, we discover to our astonishment that the search for suitable alternatives offers too many directions in which to flee, and therefore none at all, since all voices are equally marginalized by the marginalization of God's Son. So when Heinrich Bullinger, for example, confidently asserts *Praedicatio verbi Dei est verbum Dei*—"The preaching of the Word of God *is* the Word of God"[7]—we must qualify the possibly triumphalist overtones of his claim by listening more penitently to the theology of his contemporary Martin Luther, and in particular to Luther's theology of the cross, according to which no human word may dare usurp the role that belongs to God's word alone.

There is good news in this scenario, especially so for preachers who are otherwise liable to slide by imperceptible degrees toward assuming the importance of their own mediatorial role in proclaiming divine truth to passive or semi-passive recipients. The silence of God's incarnate word announces our liberation, not only in a specifically soteriological sense, but also in the broader sense that it represents the death of our religious aspirations in general, nullifying our attempt to offer an adequate human response to God. Above all for preachers, it obviates the careful religious

---

6. On the implications for preaching of the silence of the cross, see further Knowles, *We Preach Not Ourselves*, 24, 261–62.

7. *Confessio Helvetica Posterior* I, 4 (the Second Helvetic Confession of 1566), quoted in Greidanus, *The Modern Preacher and the Ancient Text*, 9.

rhetoric that endeavors by its own cleverness to pronounce an authoritative, even definitive word concerning God.[8] Thus freed from such a humanly impossible task, Christian proclamation assumes more manageable dimensions as responsible *testimony* to the things of God.[9] Preaching is always a characteristically responsive task whose actions depend on the initiative of God, and whose concepts reflect the theological precedent and priority of the *missio dei*. In just such terms, again writing to the church at Corinth, Paul characterizes himself as no more than a messenger whose role is determined by the nature of the word he must convey. To borrow from Eugene Peterson's lively paraphrase: "Remember, our Message is not about ourselves; we're proclaiming Jesus Christ, the Master. All we are is messengers, errand runners from Jesus for you."[10] By implication, proclaiming "Jesus Christ as Lord" (Ἰησοῦν Χριστὸν κύριον) includes an acknowledgment of Christ's supremacy even over the very proclamation that concerns him. Even words *about* Christ are governed by the triumph *of* Christ.

In short, the possibility of cross-cultural preaching begins with the historical particularity of Jesus of Nazareth, the definitive theological character of which relativizes all other cultural moments. The supra-cultural nature of theology in principle and the counter-cultural implications of Jesus' crucifixion together redefine the role of subsequent human agency in proclaiming the things of God, whether at the level of language, worldview, and social custom, or as concerns the task of the individual preacher.

Babel and Pentecost: The Tongues of Men and Angels

Although the significance of the respective narratives can hardly be reduced to single dimensions, I propose that the contrasting models of Babel and Pentecost, which lie on either side of the theological watershed that is Jesus' crucifixion and resurrection, together encapsulate many of the dynamics at play in cross-cultural preaching. On the one hand, there is Babel, a marvel of human achievement that deploys cutting-edge technology in the service of legitimate and pressing human need (Gen 11:1–9). It is a project undertaken by migrants, nomads "from the East" who arrive on the plain

---

8. See further Purves, *Reconstructing Pastoral Theology*, 156–60.

9. This theological category is given contemporary shape by Ricoeur's essay, "The Hermeneutics of Testimony"; cf. Long, *Witness of Preaching*, 46–51.

10. From Peterson, *The Message*, 2 Cor 4:5.

of Shinar looking for a place to settle down and call their own. After the manner of Abraham and his kind generations later, they are "strangers and exiles on the earth," people "seeking a homeland" (Heb 11:14–15) who are motivated by alienation, rootlessness, instability, and the desire for security that only common cause and community can remedy. The builders' self description is telling: "Come," they say, "let us build a *city*, and a *tower* and let us make a *name* for ourselves; otherwise we shall be scattered abroad upon the face of the whole earth." As a technological innovation, they burn clay to make bricks, and bind them with petroleum tar for mortar, so as to construct a city with a sacred precinct in its midst. Their crowning achievement is not a tower intended to "storm heaven," as commentators at least as far back as Augustine (*City of God* 16.4) have proposed, but more likely a ziggurat with sacred temples at its base and summit (if Herodotus, *Histories* 1.181–183, is to be believed). They do not intend independence from God so much as to create suitable conditions for the divine-human encounter. Their solution to the insecurity of human existence is to harness technology and ingenuity in the service of popular theology.

It turns out that God is both impressed by their achievement and alarmed by its implications:

> And the LORD said, "Look, they are one people, and they have all one language; and this is only the beginning of what they will do; nothing that they propose to do will now be impossible for them. Come, let us go down, and confuse their language there, so that they will not understand one another's speech." So the LORD scattered them abroad from there over the face of all the earth, and they left off building the city (Gen 11:6–8).

Our familiarity with this story must not be allowed to obscure its theological import. According to Genesis 11, the details of language and culture that so divide us, so frustrate the task of preaching, are an initial divine response to the human desire for community, identity, and security. These are immigrants who only want to make a name for themselves, to secure their own future. Their project entails not simply making room for God, but establishing times and places and liturgies and sacred precincts for God, creating the proper conditions for heaven and earth to meet. In short, they endeavor to co-opt God as a remedy for human need.

With the noblest of intentions, it is an error that we have faithfully replicated ever since. To speak of God we must use *this* language, not that; at *this* time, rather than some other hour; in *this* place, and not elsewhere.

Whether in Greek, Latin, or King James English; in my denomination or tradition rather than yours; using this liturgy, in my house of worship, led by this set of duly ordered clergy, with or without the help of PowerPoint and video clips: these are the terms and conditions whereby God is best met, for we each invariably know ourselves to be closer to the truth than those who do things differently. Preachers recognize themselves at once in the "light bulb" joke that applies to their profession: "How many preachers does it take to change a light bulb?" Answer: "Only one, but I could have done it better."

Jesus tells a parable about a man who set out to build a tower, but lacked the wherewithal to complete his task and thereby earned the scorn of all who saw it (Luke 14:28-30). Perhaps in our case it is none other than God who looks down from heaven and scoffs. The parable concludes, "In the same way, those of you who do not give up everything you have cannot be my disciples" (Luke 14:33; TNIV). Why should that injunction not apply equally to the act of preaching, cross-cultural or otherwise? Jesus' own ministry ends in crucifixion, a far cry from what his followers expected. The apostles' dreams of glory are thereby dashed, and they go back to fishing. Preachers have no right to anticipate a more congenial turn of events.

Still, the confusion of languages and the failure of human piety are by no means the end of the gospel story. At least as interpreted here, the narrative of the first tower builders and God's defeat of their well-intentioned project—the recognition that no one community, no single language or culture has a monopoly on the divine—is no more than a prelude to the eventual dimensions of God's intended outcome. In the salvation-historical course of things, crushed hope is unexpectedly fulfilled: crucifixion is counter-balanced by resurrection; the stunned silence of disappointed faith is reversed by testimony to a triumph that only God could have accomplished; confusion resolves into comprehension. For the disciples themselves, the guilt and shame of having failed their Messiah are effaced by the generosity of his greeting: "Peace be with you" (John 20:19, 21). The risen Jesus meets his followers beside a defeated tomb, in an upper room, on the road to Emmaus, atop a mountain, on a lakeside beach. Then and only then, as Luke tells it, he commissions them to a ministry of cross-cultural preaching, as witnesses "to all nations." But rather than sending them on their way now that their task is plain, he tells them to do nothing until they have been "clothed with power from on high" (Luke 24:46-49). This too constitutes clear testimony to the futility of unaided human endeavor in accomplishing the purposes of God, even as it announces the disciples' pivotal role in just such a task.

Pentecost is the theological counterpoint to Babel. With human pretension—human presumption—soundly defeated at the cross, God alone sets the terms and conditions for human testimony regarding things divine. If Babel is familiar, the story of Pentecost is even more so. Still, it is worth pausing to reflect on the significance of one or two details. The first of these is the careful balance between diversity of language and culture, on the one hand, and the universal character of Christ's salvation, on the other. Here, the unity and security for which we long are not achieved by some act of human ingenuity or self-affirmation. On the contrary, they represent an act of reversal, a divine gift in the sending of the Spirit who enables Jesus' followers to bear witness to what God has accomplished in the face of human obstinacy and incomprehension:

> All of them were filled with the Holy Spirit and began to speak in other languages, as the Spirit gave them ability . . . At this sound the crowd gathered and was bewildered, because each one heard them speaking in the native language of each. Amazed and astonished, they asked, "Are not all these who are speaking Galileans? And how is it that we hear, each of us, in our own native language? . . . in our own languages we hear them speaking about God's deeds of power" (Acts 2:4, 6–8, 11).

To tease apart various theological strands that weave through this story, we may observe, first, how the defeated disciples are empowered to speak of divine reversal in such a way that the cultural identities of those who hear them are simultaneously affirmed and transcended. As Newbigin observes, "Pentecost is our biblical warrant for saying that God accepts languages."[11] Sri Lankan theologian Vinoth Ramachandra expands on the radical implications of this principle:

> What has distinguished the Christian movement from, say, the ancient Asian religions or global Islam is the way, from its inception, the church did not sacralize either the language of Jesus [or] the place of his origins. The language that Jesus used in his preaching was quickly abandoned in favor of country (Koine) Greek and "vulgar" Latin as the uniting media of communication. The entire New Testament was written in a language other than the one in which Jesus preached. That the eternal counsels of God belonged

---

11. Newbigin, *Gospel in a Pluralist Society*, 185.

to the commonplace, everyday speech of ordinary men and women was a view that was, and remains, revolutionary.[12]

Each in their own language hears testimony to the "mighty acts of God (τὰ μεγαλεῖα τοῦ θεοῦ)," which in this context can only indicate the work of Christ.[13] Yet here diversity of linguistic expression serves a function precisely opposite that which obtained on the plain of Shinar. Grace that once divided human language now reconciles those divisions: as Saint Cyril of Jerusalem (ca. 315–387) astutely observes by way of contrast between Babel and Pentecost, "Through what occasioned the fall came the recovery."[14] Solomon Avotri offers a modern African reading of Babel as an attempt by God to remain distant and largely inaccessible to humanity.[15] But even if we grant this interpretation (which is by no means certain), surely the story of Pentecost presents a striking resolution to all such estrangement. Their Spirit-inspired speech offers unifying testimony to an act of human and divine reconciliation, paradoxically resolving the barriers of language even in the course of acknowledging them. As the disciples yield to the initiative of the Spirit, a new human community assumes its proper identity as a concrete, living witness to the reconciling initiative of God. This is the first act of the infant church, encapsulating in a single moment the essential character of its theological identity.

Peter's sermon immediately following sounds the same note:

> This is what was spoken through the prophet Joel: "In the last days it will be, God declares, that I will pour out my Spirit upon all flesh, and your sons and your daughters shall prophesy, and your young men shall see visions, and your old men shall dream dreams. Even upon my slaves, both men and women, in those days I will pour out my Spirit; and they shall prophesy" (Acts 2:16–18).

---

12. Ramachandra, *Subverting Global Myths*, 133. Ramachandra (147) quotes West African scholar Lamin Sanneh on this point: "The fact of Christianity being a translated, and translating, religion places God at the center of the universe of cultures, implying free coequality among cultures and a necessary relativizing of languages vis-à-vis the truth of God. No culture is so advanced and so superior that it can claim exclusive access or advantage to the truth of God, and none is so marginal or inferior that it can be excluded" (Sanneh, *Whose Religion Is Christianity*, 105–6).

13. So Grundmann, "μεγαλεῖον," 541; for Lucan usage with reference to God, cf. Luke 1:49; 9:43.

14. *Catechetical Lecture* 17.17, in McCauley and Stephenson, *Works of Saint Cyril of Jerusalem*, II.107.

15. Avotri, "Genesis 11:1–9," 17–23.

The Globalization of Christianity

In his commentary on this passage, the eighth-century Anglo-Saxon historian known as the Venerable Bede (*ca.* 673–735) remarks that "the grace of the Holy Spirit was not to be granted, as formerly, only to individual prophets and priests, but to everyone in every place, regardless of sex, state of life, or position."[16] Young and old; male and female; slave and freeborn: no more than language, culture, or ethnicity can such distinctions now determine the contours of the divine-human encounter. Such breadth of address explains why Luke recounts a new outpouring of the same Spirit upon the Samaritans (Acts 8:14–17), then subsequently upon the first Gentile believers (10:44–46); each time, the testimony to God's saving work fords a new boundary of language, culture, or religious identity.

In short, cross-cultural preaching modeled after the book of Acts acknowledges the inescapable reality of linguistic and cultural identity, while at the same time testifying to a divine initiative that resolves the divisive character of these very distinctions. In just this sense, Paul can declare to the church of Galatia, "There is no longer Jew or Greek, there is no longer slave or free, there is no longer male and female; for all of you are one in Christ Jesus" (Gal 3:28). From a certain perspective, of course, he is quite mistaken, for critical distinctions of gender, race, economic circumstance, social location, individual liberty, and self-determination endure to our day, in many cases regrettably so. But the apostle's intended meaning—his cross-cultural testimony—is that such distinctions are no longer absolute or determinative for those who find their primary identity "in Christ." Because these divisions have been relativized by the cultural specificity of the Incarnation, moderated and minimized by the religious disaster that is the crucifixion, then ultimately transcended by the resurrection that inaugurates a new creation, they no longer serve as pre-conditions, one way or another, for human access to God. This is why Peter quotes Joel in his Pentecost sermon to the effect that "*all* who call on the name of the Lord will be saved," and why he concludes by insisting that "the promise is for you and your children and for *all* who are far off—for *all* whom the Lord our God will call" (Acts 2:21, 39; TNIV). In all three cases the "all" is both theologically and homiletically all-important. Similar language anchors the exposition of Christ's saving accomplishment in the letter to the Ephesians:

> But now in Christ Jesus you who once were far off have been brought near by the blood of Christ. For he is our peace; in his flesh he has made both groups into one and has broken down the

---

16. Bede, *Commentary on the Acts of the Apostles*, 32.

> dividing wall, that is, the hostility between us.... So he came and proclaimed peace [εὐηγγελίσατο εἰρήνην] to you who were far off and peace to those who were near; for through him both of us have access in one Spirit to the Father (Eph 2:13-14, 17-18; NRSV).

The point to be noted here is the direct parallel between the peacemaking proclamation of Christ and that of the writer, whose task is likewise to proclaim reconciliation to Gentiles otherwise excluded from the saving purposes of God:

> Although I am less than the least of all the Lord's people, this grace was given to me to preach [εὐαγγελίσασθαι] to the Gentiles the boundless riches of Christ ... In him and through faith in him we may approach God with freedom and confidence (Eph 3:8, 12; TNIV).

Preaching across Cultural Divides

The foregoing discussion prompts the following summative observations regarding the theological character—what might be termed the theological *method*—of cross-cultural preaching. First, and paradoxically, cross-cultural preaching communicates in language that not only makes sense to the hearers, but also honors the particular dimensions of their human situation. It is sensitive to nuances of social location, cultural context, linguistic expression, and national identity. It speaks in recognizable terms of a God who chose to become humanly recognizable in the person of Jesus of Nazareth.

Second, it points, at the same time, beyond all human languages, social locations, and cultural identities, in its testimony to the "mighty acts of God" accomplished by that same historically-specific Jesus. It addresses issues of cultural specificity by directing attention instead to the cultural specificity of the Incarnation, by which God has reconciled all things to himself. In so doing, cross-cultural preaching takes special care to point beyond its own agency to the agency of God. It remains acutely sensitive to the idolatry of human religiosity, the all-too-human tendency to constrain God's power and limit God's availability to "people like us." Rather than absolutizing the ecclesiastical dimensions of our own social location, this sort of preaching acknowledges that we are not in a position to dictate the terms and conditions of the divine-human encounter. It endeavors to keep silent long enough to hear a voice not of its own articulating.

Accordingly, third, this sort of theologically astute proclamation consciously relies on the enablement of the Holy Spirit, penitently acknowledging the futility of our own desire to mediate between God and our listeners, joining them rather in their status as simple recipients and stewards of the grace of God. It appropriates the theological perspective of the Johannine prologue, "To all who received him, who believed in his name, he gave power to become children of God, who were born, *not* of blood *nor* of the will of the flesh *nor* of the will of man, but of God" (John 1:12–13), and of Paul's curt dismissal of the methods employed by his opponents and detractors: "the kingdom of God depends not on talk but on power" (1 Cor 4:20).

Fourth, in keeping with the previous two points, cross-cultural preaching is properly characterized as "cruciform." It takes, to be sure, its theological cue primarily from the historical circumstances of Jesus' human ministry, its fateful abrogation and ultimate vindication. But methodologically, it also is intentionally cruciform in its conscious imitation of Jesus' own orientation toward God, yielding all prerogatives of human power so as to rely instead on the power of God. This is the posture Paul adopts:

> I came to you in weakness and in fear and in much trembling. My speech and my proclamation were not with plausible words of wisdom, but with a demonstration of the Spirit and of power, so that your faith might rest not on human wisdom but on the power of God (1 Cor 2:3–5).

As Michael Gorman notes, "Paul explicitly avers that his lack of rhetorical polish and ornamentation insure that the Corinthians' response to his preaching is the work of divine power, the power of the cross, not human intellect or emotional, rhetorical manipulation."[17]

Fifth, our cross-cultural proclamation acknowledges, without endeavoring to resolve, the constant tension that exists between each particular enculturation of the saving word and its relativization according to the universal dimensions of the *missio dei*. It therefore, of necessity, remains humbly open to correction in light of other perspectives and cultural appropriations. Specifically, it remains inescapably caught between the "once for all" of first-century Palestine, on the one hand, and the universal implications of a "new creation," on the other. The preaching of the New Testament moves back and

---

17. Gorman, *Cruciformity*, 283.

forth between the Bethlehemite "Emmanuel" of Matthew's Gospel and the worship of "every tribe and tongue" that fills the book of Revelation.

Finally, sixth, cross-cultural preaching of the sort described here bears witness to and thereby represents an extension of God's gracious work of reconciliation, as a re-ordering of human identity in all its dimensions. Even at risk to their own security (professional as much as personal), preachers of a cross-cultural gospel dare to challenge every hegemony of culture or class, technology or power, nation or race. They offer an alternative, divinely-authored solution to the alienation, rootlessness, and social dislocation that every assertion of linguistic and political absolutism seeks in its own way to remedy.

The Irony of Preaching

In the last analysis, preaching is a profoundly ironic gesture. To all appearances, it consists of human words addressed to human hearers. Yet particularly when human speech attempts to negotiate the interconnected nexus of cultural, linguistic, and conceptual boundaries, the limitations inherent in all human self-expression come quickly to the fore. Conceiving of Christian proclamation rather as a process of listening—both to the voices of other listeners, and above all to the word of God—offers a fruitful resolution to this dilemma, as well as a practical way forward. In this view, what appears on the surface to be an act of human communication may be reconfigured as an act of willful submission to the words of Another, and to God's paradoxical willingness to communicate through us what human words alone cannot express. Knowing that words cannot of themselves fully articulate, much less effect, the reconciliation that God intends, preachers bear witness instead to a word—a λόγος τοῦ σταυροῦ—that is greater than their own attempts at Christian speech. More especially, they intentionally yield to the power of the Spirit of God, whose testimony through them places both culture and language in proper perspective, reconciling speakers and hearers alike by focusing instead on the work of Christ. Preaching is ironic because it is not what it first seems; precisely for this reason, in knowing itself to depend on more than its own words, Christian proclamation bears faithful witness to the resolution of cultural boundaries made possible in Christ.

Bibliography

Avotri, Solomon. "Genesis 11:1–9: An African Perspective." In *Return to Babel: Global Perspectives on the Bible*, edited by John R. Levison and Priscilla Pope-Levison, 17–25. Louisville: Westminster John Knox, 1999.

Bede, Saint. *Commentary on the Acts of the Apostles*. Translated by Lawrence T. Martin. Cistercian Studies 117. Kalamazoo, MI: Cistercian, 1989.

Gorman, Michael J. *Cruciformity: Paul's Narrative Spirituality of the Cross*. Grand Rapids: Eerdmans, 2001.

Greidanus, Sidney. *The Modern Preacher and the Ancient Text: Interpreting and Preaching Biblical Literature*. Grand Rapids: Eerdmans, 1988.

Grundmann, Walter. S.v. μεγαλεῖον. In *TDNT* 4:541.

Jenkins, Philip. *The Lost History of Christianity: The Thousand-Year Golden Age of the Church in the Middle East, Africa, and Asia—and How It Died*. New York: HarperCollins, 2008.

———. *The New Faces of Christianity: Believing the Bible in the Global South*. New York: Oxford University Press, 2006.

Knowles, Michael P. *We Preach Not Ourselves: Paul on Proclamation*. Grand Rapids: Brazos, 2008.

Long, Thomas G. *The Witness of Preaching*. 2nd ed. Louisville: Westminster John Knox, 2005.

McCauley, Leo P., and Anthony A. Stephenson, trans. *The Works of Saint Cyril of Jerusalem*. Fathers of the Church 64. Washington: Catholic University of America Press, 1970.

Meconi, David Vincent. "Silence Proceeding." *Logos: A Journal of Catholic Thought and Culture* 5, no. 2 (2002) 59–75.

Newbigin, Lesslie. *The Gospel in a Pluralist Society*. Grand Rapids: Eerdmans, 1989.

Peterson, Eugene H. *The Message: The New Testament in Contemporary English*. Colorado Springs: NavPress, 1993.

Purves, Andrew. *Reconstructing Pastoral Theology: A Christological Foundation*. Louisville: Westminster John Knox, 2004.

Ramachandra, Vinoth. *Subverting Global Myths: Theology and the Public Issues Shaping Our World*. Downers Grove, IL: IVP Academic, 2008.

Ricoeur, Paul. "The Hermeneutics of Testimony." In *Essays on Biblical Interpretation*, edited by Lewis S. Mudge, 119–54. Translated by David Stewart and Paul Reagan. Philadelphia: Fortress, 1980.

Sanneh, Lamin. *Whose Religion Is Christianity? The Gospel beyond the West*. Grand Rapids: Eerdmans, 2003.

6

Soaking Prayer and the Advancement of the Kingdom of Love
Charismatic Renewal as Mission

Peter Althouse and Michael Wilkinson

> If you want to fulfill the Great Commission, you have to be very highly involved in the Great Commandment. Without knowing that you're a son instead of an orphan, you're going to try and validate what you do through your ministry, through recognition, through all kinds of other stuff that is actually not very healthy... Being motivated because we're in love is incomparable to being motivated by anything else.
>
> —SOAKING PRAYER PARTICIPANT 28[1]

IN 1994, A REVIVAL broke out in a small Vineyard Church in the west end of Toronto near Pearson International Airport. This seemingly inauspicious event first gained media attention for the ecstatic phenomena of laughing, weeping, animal noises, involuntary falling, and other ecstatic ritual behavior associated with the charismatic renewal. The British press dubbed the revival the Toronto Blessing, and John and Carol Arnott became high profile charismatic exemplars in the Pentecostal-Charismatic world. Christian

---

1. In research for this chapter, interviews were conducted with 126 participants. The number 28 refers to the 28th participant in our interviews.

pilgrims travelled to Toronto from around the world to witness this new movement of the Spirit. They represented a range of Christian denominations including Anglican, Roman Catholic, Reformed, classical Pentecostal, and a host of others. Soon after the revival began, the Vineyard severed its ties with the Toronto church. The church responded immediately by changing its name to Toronto Airport Christian Fellowship, establishing relationships with other denominational pastors and leaders through an organizational network called Friends in Harvest, forming institutional structures in an organization called Partners in Harvest, and networking with other charismatic leaders. While most people thought the revival had declined and virtually disappeared by 1998, two years of observations reveal that this is not the case, as the organization continues to grow and expand. Since 2010, a new global charismatic ministry network has become well established, known as Catch the Fire (CTF). As leaders of CTF, John and Carol Arnott remain influential members in the apostolic network, conducting major conferences with charismatic leaders such as Heidi Baker, Randy Clarke, Che Ahn, Bill Johnson, and others.

CTF has developed an extensive prayer movement spreading throughout the world, focusing on experiencing what they claim to be "the Father's love" through "soaking prayer." Soaking prayer is a type of meditative prayer in which one stills the mind and "rests," often with worship music in the background, in order to soak in the love of the Father. In the early stages of the renewal, people would fall down spontaneously in a phenomenon called "resting in the Spirit" and playfully called "carpet time." CTF leaders, however, ritualized the practice so that people did not have to wait for God to "knock them down," but could lie down on the floor, usually with pillows and blankets, and wait on God. Soaking prayer sustains the experience of divine love and presence for participants and allows them to experience the "signs and wonders" of renewal. In the United States, CTF claims to have over 500 soaking centers in homes and churches, and has developed networking structures with regional soaking prayer coordinators. About 150 of these centers have officially registered with CTF. These soaking centers are not confined to any one specific denomination, but spill into Anglican/Episcopal, Roman Catholic, Vineyard, Assemblies of God, Baptist, and independent charismatic churches, who either host, or at least accept, soaking prayer as part of their ministry.[2]

---

2. This chapter is based upon our research on soaking prayer in the charismatic renewal. A John Templeton grant through the "Flame of Love" project funded our research.

Soaking Prayer and the Advancement of the Kingdom of Love

CTF leaders understand their history in three stages: gathering, scattering, and sending. The gathering stage was the period of the early renewal when people would travel to Toronto and the church had to develop facilities and resources to accommodate these pilgrims. The scattering stage was the period when pilgrimages to Toronto dwindled, but participants were inserting the charismatic experiences and values back into their own churches and communities. During this stage, the leaders were happy to share their message with any who wanted to hear it, but the process was haphazard and lacked organizational focus. The sending stage is the current period in CTF's history, when leaders are intentional in spreading the renewal through the packaging of its core values and teachings in order to spread the renewal throughout the world. The manifestation of the kingdom of God in this world is an important belief. Signs and wonders are indicators of the kingdom's presence and are equated with the presence of the Father's love. Christians are encouraged to participate in the kingdom's expansion through the expression of love in benevolent behavior.

This chapter examines the relationship between prayer, love, and CTF's mission strategy. CTF's vision statement reads: "Our vision is to walk in God's love and give it away, until the whole earth is filled with the knowledge of the glory of the Lord."[3]

Its mission is to spread the Father's love to all the churches and throughout the world in order to manifest the kingdom of God on the earth, as it is in heaven. CTF's mission, however, is tied to the Great Commandment, which is to love God with all your heart, mind, body, and soul and then to love your neighbor as yourself (Matt 22:37, 39; Mark 12:30–31; Luke 10:27). According to informants' claims, through the reception of the Father's love in soaking prayer, participants are energized and motivated to engage in benevolent care of others in the world. This activity can range in scope from showing more love to spouses and family members to extensive ministries of compassion, social transformation, and social justice. To explore the relationship between prayer, love, and mission, we offer a theoretical framework from the sociology of love that seeks to understand the relationship between love and action. We then consider how CTF understands the relationship between prayer, love, and mission. Finally, we

---

Our findings are based on a survey of charismatics, involving two years of fieldwork, formal interviews with over 126 participants, and site observations. For a full discussion of our research, see Wilkinson and Althouse, *Catch the Fire*.

3. http://www.catchthefire.com/about/vision-mission-values, accessed May 25, 2014.

engage in a theological assessment of current discussions on mission in order to offer a proposal that views charismatic renewal as mission.

Love in Action: A Theoretical Framework for Interactional Love

A number of theoretical considerations inform our investigation. These include the work of Harvard sociologist Pitirim Sorokin, who established an empirical agenda for the examination of love, and the work of Margaret Poloma, Stephen Post, Matthew Lee, and Ralph Hood, Jr., who developed an interactional model of love that they identify as "godly love."

Sorokin made the most extensive contribution in sociology for understanding altruism as benevolent acts of love in his book *The Ways and Power of Love*. His work focused on establishing a framework for the type of scientific work on love he proposed. Sorokin attempted to establish a definition of love. However, he did not work from the premise that a single definition was universally useful. Rather, following a more integrative approach, he developed a multifaceted approach acknowledging a range of ways to think about love, including the religious, ethical, ontological, physical, biological, psychological, and social. Keeping in mind the multi-dimensions of love, Sorokin then moved on to develop the psychological and social qualities, outlining a range of empirical dimensions for measuring love including its intensity, extensity, duration, purity, and adequacy. He also focused on what he called "Apostles of love" or the exemplars of love, who included key historical figures like Jesus, Buddha, Ghandi, and Albert Schweitzer.[4] What Sorokin examined was how each of these figures was able to transcend the hostilities of their time, not only by focusing on those outside their ethnic, tribal, or political group, but also by establishing an important link to what Sorokin called the supraconscious, a source of greater love that motivates loving action or altruistic behavior.

Finally, Sorokin explored a variety of techniques by which exemplars over time have become energized by love and hence able to love others more deeply. In particular, he paid attention to the techniques of yoga, meditation, and prayer. He insisted that love could transform the social world and ultimately humanity itself. He focused on rituals associated with prayer including meditation, silence, and mystical encounters, and wrote:

---

4. Sorokin, *Ways and Power of Love*, 127.

> Prayer is a most sincere communion of the individual with his highest self, or soul, or God, or with the Supreme Cosmic Power. However conceived—and they are conceived differently by different persons, groups, and cultures—this self, or soul, or God, or the Supreme Cosmic Being is always intuited as something far transcending the individual in power, wisdom, glory, creativity, goodness, and other insights.[5]

"Prayer," he argues, "serves as a marvelous road for a pilgrimage to the magnificent peaks of spirituality and altruism."[6]

Sorokin's work underlies an important aspect of our understanding of the experience of soaking prayer and what charismatics call "the Father's love." Specifically, we pay attention to the techniques by which people come to experience love, or what Sorokin calls a process of altruization or altruistic transformation. Soaking prayer is a specific type of prayer among charismatic Christians that focuses on resting, receiving, and experiencing divine love. Those who practice soaking prayer also have high levels of altruistic behavior demonstrated by a range of loving acts towards others. Sorokin observed that an outflow of love depended upon an inflow of love and he included the value of experiences with a divine source of love in his understanding. Love is a kind of energy that infuses people, motivating and leading them to meaningful acts. On the social level, Sorokin defined love as "a meaningful interaction—or relationship—between two or more persons where the aspirations and aims of one person are shared and helped in their realization by other persons."[7] These ideas shape our assumptions about soaking prayer and the charismatic experience of the Father's love.

While Sorokin offers a theoretical framework for understanding and studying the relationship between love and prayer, his work has not been used extensively until recently. Margaret Poloma has long been concerned with several themes in her research on Pentecostal-Charismatic Christianity, especially the institutionalization of religion, religious experience, religious revitalization, and, more recently, what she calls "godly love." For our purposes, we focus on her most recent contributions as they pertain to the development of the godly love model.

Poloma conducted extensive research on the Toronto blessing, including several years of participant observation, surveys, and formal interviews

---

5. Ibid., 334.
6. Ibid., 335–36.
7. Ibid., 13.

that she published as *Main Street Mystics: The Toronto Blessing and Reviving Pentecostalism*. She argued that even classical Pentecostals needed renewal, and that it had come through this new revival where people were experiencing profound spiritual transformations. Although it was not the major focus of the book, Poloma made several initial observations about the importance among the leaders of the Toronto Blessing given to love, encountering the Father's love, and loving others. She noted that social scientists were reluctant to speak about love and certainly did not investigate the relationship between experiences of divine love among religious people and consequential social action or benevolence. Charismatics, it seems, were tapping into something important and this experience of love, she thought, might be central for understanding how mission and ministry may be shaped by divine love.[8] This question about love and its relationship to religious organizations and revitalization soon became a central focus in her research agenda.

In 2008, Margaret Poloma, Stephen Post, and Matthew Lee were awarded a John Templeton grant to explore the role of love and revitalization among Pentecostal-Charismatic Christians. The study was called the "Flame of Love Project" and set out to examine the following: "To what extent can emotionally powerful experiences of a 'divine flame of love' move us beyond our ordinary self-interests and help us express unconditional, unlimited love for all others, especially when our human capacities seem to reach their limits?"[9] A number of collaborators were invited to participate in the study, including the authors of this essay, and over a two-year period we investigated the role of soaking prayer and the experience of love among charismatics. The model of "godly love" has been developed as a result of Poloma's research on the Pentecostal-Charismatic movement that highlights a range of interactional relationships for the experience, production, and expression of love.

In *A Sociological Study of the Great Commandment in Pentecostalism*, Matthew Lee and Margaret Poloma further developed the sociology of love in an examination of findings from 101 exemplars and collaborators—people who practiced love in some form of benevolent service. The authors argued that the concept of godly love is not a synonym for experiencing

---

8. Poloma, *Main Street Mystics*, 140–41.

9. See http://www.templeton.org/what-we-fund/grants/the-flame-of-love-scientific-research-on-the-experience-and-expression-of-godly-, accessed May 25, 2014. The quote and a discussion of the project can be found in Lee, Poloma and Post, "Introduction," 5.

God's love. Rather, the idea of "godly love" was conceptually developed to capture a range of interactions between individuals and God on a vertical axis and between individuals and the numerous people, organizations, and communities on a horizontal axis that are the recipients of benevolent service. This interaction is captured in the "diamond model" of godly love that consists of the divine at the top end of the model, and exemplars, collaborators, and beneficiaries interacting with each other in numerous ways. This model attempts to take seriously the perceptions of the divine-human interaction by the various human actors within the range of social interactions. From our perspective, "godly love" is a methodological tool devised to "see" social phenomena for understanding love and religious altruism among charismatics. The interaction of love in our qualitative observations is specifically articulated and practiced among CTF participants as "the Father's love" and has a range of meanings for charismatic Christians. The Father's love, conceptually, derives from our use of grounded theory methodology, in which research concepts arise from the data of participant observation.[10]

Finally, Margaret Poloma and John C. Green published *The Assemblies of God: Godly Love and the Revitalization of American Pentecostalism*. The authors explored in detail the role of love as a possible means for revitalization within the Assemblies of God (AG). Poloma and Green re-examined the dilemmas of institutionalization and discovered that while many remained, there were also signs of renewal, especially among those where love was evident. In places in the AG where institutionalization had had a detrimental effect, Poloma and Green observed signs of revitalization, noting high levels of experiential love and the corresponding outcome of benevolence. The model presented by Poloma and Green offers a conceptual orientation for exploring the relationships among institutionalization, prayer, experiences of divine love, and benevolence.

Of importance for our research on CTF is the argument that institutionalizing does not necessarily mean certain death for a given religious organization. Institutionalization may be an impediment for accomplishing any number of objectives, and especially an organization's mission. However, institutionalization may also preserve an organization's mission and identity, with moments of renewal leading to fresh experiences and commitments to its objectives. Despite the rapid institutionalization that is

---

10. See Glaser and Strauss, *Discovery of Grounded Theory*; Charmaz, *Constructing Grounded Theory*.

occurring, there is evidence that ecstatic charismatic phenomena are still a major part of CTF and fuel much of its global expansion.

Rolf M. Johnson's typology of love is the most helpful for our own framing of love in the charismatic renewal.[11] He proposes three types of love: union-love, care-love, and appreciative-love. Union-love seeks to diminish the distance between lovers in order to merge and unite them and this type includes the mystical kinds of love that one sees in ecstatic Christianity, including the charismatic renewal. Care-love embraces all forms of concern for the other, including but not limited to those associated with love of neighbor. Different kinds of social action, altruism, and benevolent behavior are included in care-love. Appreciative-love constitutes the affirmation, appreciation, and acceptance of the object of love. While union-love involves a more intense range of passions, appreciative-love is more detached. While care-love is more ethical in its formulation, appreciative-love is more aesthetic.[12] Union-love and care-love especially are observed in the various interactions of the charismatic renewal associated with CTF.

Advancing the Kingdom through Soaking Prayer

Soaking prayer has become the preferred ritual practice among CTF charismatics that facilitates the reception of love and its expression to others. The Father's love is claimed to be experienced through prayer so that the participant is full of love, and this love energy is given away to others in acts of love. Soaking prayer has also become important in the expansion of the charismatic renewal that CTF leaders see as coinciding with the advancement of the kingdom. With the development of soaking prayer schools, soaking kits, and teaching materials, CTF has either established or partnered with soaking prayer centers in seventy-two countries throughout the world. Through soaking centers, CTF has developed a religious network through which its teaching and core values can be propagated. Most recently, soaking prayer centers have facilitated the development of new church plants in and around the greater Toronto area. These churches have become satellites of CTF Toronto. However, the practice of soaking prayer itself, which includes inward, upward, and outward components, is the primary means by which charismatics experience and express love.

---

11. Johnson, *Three Faces of Love*, 102–108.
12. Ibid., 23–26; and throughout.

Soaking Prayer and the Advancement of the Kingdom of Love

In February 2011 we attended a Catch the Fire Conference held at Founders Inn in Virginia Beach. Speaking to a full capacity crowd, John Arnott began with a specific address to the internet audience. He proclaimed, "We are all players in the kingdom," and prayed "God right now bring your kingdom and bring miracles." A short time later, Arnott gave a message that he has given many times at different conferences on the inward, upward, and outward focus of prayer.

The inward focus is to be embraced by God, to be forgiven and to forgive, to be healed and carry the character of Jesus Christ, and "to embrace the values of the kingdom of God."[13] The inward is about character so that an even greater anointing can be carried in the expansion of God's kingdom. Arnott said, "[God] wants us to be gathered in the Father's love."[14] The importance of the inward is "not the manifestation or the power that is part of the ministry, but the deep revelation of the Father's love."[15]

The upward focus is not about us but about God and relating to him. It focuses on the Father heart of God. "This is the upward relationship in that it is not about going to heaven but about being with the Father. While many are afraid of the Father because of their fear of judgment, the Father is the life that Jesus expressed."[16] Drawing on Eph 3:17–20, Arnott urged the audience to prepare their hearts to fall in love with the King of Kings and Lord of Lords. "The Father says, 'I really love who you are.' A lot of culture really does not understand how love works."[17]

The outward focus is "carrying the anointing and blessing into the harvest field or the mission field."[18] Arnott then talked about the kingdom of God as a kingdom of love and its expansion as an expression of love, captured in charismatic anointing. He spoke about how people need to be healed of their hurts and deal with their issues until they have experienced the Father's heart. "The revelation of the Father's heart is essential in order to know that He really loves you. He loves you the way you are, but loves you too much to leave you as you are."[19] Arnott went on to say that the Holy Spirit is the motor, the divine force of all that equipping.

13. Arnott, "Opening Message."
14. Ibid.
15. Ibid.
16. Ibid.
17. Ibid.
18. Ibid.
19. Ibid.

> The Holy Spirit can give you the Father's love so that you can move from being an orphan, striving and performing, to being a child, a son or daughter of God. There is a deep work that God wants to do in our hearts to set us free to be in relationship with God. God's presence brings intimacy and in God's presence there's fullness of joy and enjoyment for everyone.[20]

Arnott proceeded to speak on giftedness and character and how the two must work together. He said that some churches are gifted but have no character, where others have character but no giftedness and therefore no impact.

The expansion of the kingdom of God is the theological impulse that orders CTF's mission. This kingdom is defined as a kingdom of love that impinges on the world in divine presence and charismatic renewal. The kingdom is partially realized in this world through God's relational presence in love—this is confirmed through the signs of divine presence in the form of charismatic wonders—but it remains only partial because the Father's love is not yet fully present in a world in need of it. The expansion of the kingdom is the expansion of divine love that has begun to permeate the world and continues to do so as people are equipped to carry this love to the farthest reaches of the world.

The importance of love is captured in CTF's vision: "that we may walk in the Father's love and give it away to Toronto and the world." This vision statement hangs on a banner at the back of the church in Toronto and it is used as a logo embossed on many of its products. The importance of divine love is also evidenced in CTF's core values, captured in the acronym FIRE: F—The Father's love; I—Intimacy with the Father; R—Renewal; and E—Empowering and equipping for the advancement of the kingdom. Many of CTF's conferences and events are named after different adjectival descriptions of love. Liquid Love, Intensive Love, Compelled by Love, Love Revolution, Baptism of Love, and Flame of Love[21] are some of the ways that CTF leaders describe the kind of love they experience and want to share with the world.

Participants experience divine love personally and corporately. On the personal level, the participants say that the reception of the Father's love

20. Ibid.

21. The Flame of Love Project that is funded by Templeton was named after Clark Pinnock's book by the same title. In fact, Pinnock was one of the core research members prior to his death in 2010. In a curious turn of events, after we conducted our first set of observations and interviews in 2009, the opening conference of CTF London was called "Flame of Love."

Soaking Prayer and the Advancement of the Kingdom of Love

touches the depths of the heart, body, and soul so that people who experience this love see themselves as sons and daughters who are truly loved. It includes a sense of intimacy with the Father, the realization of having been forgiven, a willingness to forgive others, and a desire to seek reconciliation. God's love is experienced as relational presence analogous to the way a husband and wife are present to each other in marriage. On the corporate level, charismatic bodies worshipping together experience this love communally. Charismatic rituals such as soaking prayer, dancing, and vocalized praise all contribute to a sense of the attunement of love energy and group solidarity, referred to as interaction ritual chains by Randall Collins.[22] The emotional energy produced through charismatic ritual contributes to a sense of being loved that can then be directed toward other social activities such as helping others, demonstrating compassion for the poor and marginalized, attempting to produce social transformation, and social justice. In other words, the perceived interactions with the divine produce a greater sense of love and compassion that can then be spent interacting with others in ways that express love and compassion. According to CTF teaching, however, one needs to be continuously filled up with the Father's love in soaking prayer to be able to share God's love with others without getting "burnt out." Put negatively, "you can't give away what you don't have," meaning that love energy expressed through benevolent ministry will be depleted unless one constantly recharges this love through prayer and renewal.

CTF places much value on the Great Commission and the Great Commandment in its view of mission. The mission of CTF is the commandment of love: "Love the Lord your God with all your heart and love your neighbor as yourself." This defines and motivates how these charismatics interact with the sacred and the mundane world. They do not love out of a sense of duty or obligation, because this would be a form of works righteousness or performance rather than grace. Instead, love flows "like a river" from a God who loves them, who wants to be present and intimate with them in relationship. It is an interaction of love made existentially real by manifestations, impartations, and signs and wonders. Once you are filled up or soaked with divine love, then you can give it away. The ordering is important; the commission of advancing the kingdom follows the relationship of love.

Advancing the kingdom is a CTF strategy for bringing the charismatic renewal into the center of Christian life. The importance of the kingdom is

---

22. Collins, *Interaction Ritual Chains*.

encapsulated in CTF's fourth value of "extending the kingdom through the equipping, anointing and empowering of the Holy Spirit," but hinges on the first two values of the Father's love and intimacy with the Father and others. Advancing the kingdom is central to the vision of CTF as the leaders seek to bring the message of the Father's love to people who are wounded and broken, to a Christian church that has lost its spiritual power, and to a world that is lost and in need of care and compassion. In theological terms, the focus of the kingdom is eschatological in an inaugural sense. One hears this in the phrases, "the kingdom of heaven is at hand," or "opening up the heavens." Advancing the kingdom by spreading the love of the Father to the world in all its charismatic manifestations is the mission of CTF.

Signs and wonders are important emphases in CTF's third value, renewal, and are related to notions of the kingdom. Central to CTF teaching is Jesus' preaching about the coming kingdom, and demonstration of its power through signs and wonders such as exorcism and healing are central to CTF teaching. The Spirit is experienced with power that advances the kingdom into new territory. One event sponsored by CTF Toronto was the "Advancing the Kingdom School," a two-day seminar held in various locations. One such "school" was held in Vancouver, British Columbia, and included sessions like "Advancing the Kingdom," "Becoming One with the Spirit of God," and "Ministering in the Power of the Holy Spirit." On the bottom of the schedule was written "Plus lots of soaking—please bring a pillow and blanket." On the first evening, John Arnott spoke about God's call to go with Jesus wherever he wants you to go. This is where charismatic Christians experience an empowerment and advance the Kingdom. "The kingdom of God must be a priority in your life," said Arnott, "but the kingdom is one of love. The fruit of the Spirit is joy, and God wants us to enjoy ourselves."[23] He then referred to the Westminster confession and reminded everyone that they are to "love God and enjoy him forever."[24] Over and over, he reminded those in attendance that the kingdom of God was about power and a demonstration of that power: "Kingdom of God come; will of God be done."[25] Arnott was preparing people for a demonstration of that power as he moved into some teaching about healing, faith, and miracles. He said, "Jesus loved the Father and the Father poured into him authority.

---

23. Arnott, "God's Call."

24. Ibid. The confession reads, "Man's chief end is to glorify God, and to enjoy him forever." *The Westminster Shorter Catechism*.

25. Arnott, "God's Call."

Soaking Prayer and the Advancement of the Kingdom of Love

Miracles happened because of the anointing. The secret of our ministry is soaking in his presence where the Holy Spirit spills over and into our lives and others."[26] Throughout his sermon he told stories of miracles from around the world. Reference was made to Luke 10, where Jesus gave power and authority to heal the sick, cast out demons, and raise the dead.

> The kingdom of God has come near you. It's a simple message. Tell people the kingdom of God is within you; reach, take hold of it. Jesus promises that the Holy Spirit will fill you. What drives your ministry? Love, not raw power. Jesus had compassion on people, loved them, filled them up on a daily basis with the love of God. He was anointed and loved others . . . The anointing of God is liquid love that flows into sickness, blindness, deafness, death.

He then transitioned to a time of prayer that included words of knowledge for healing. He emphasized that God's love is demonstrated in people's experience of emotional wholeness, forgiveness, and a greater sense of love. Charismatic signs are indicators of divine presence; God desires deep, intimate relationship. Advancing the kingdom is giving God's love away to those who are in need of it.

CHARISMATIC RENEWAL AS MISSION

The subject of mission and its practical implications for the church and the world has become an acute discussion in theological circles. One of the most important thinkers about mission is David Bosch, whose monograph *Transforming Mission* launched new directions in the theology of mission and reinvigorated discourses about the church. Bosch highlighted six paradigms of Christian mission to propose what a postmodern paradigm of mission might look like. Making a distinction between mission and missions, he argued that mission must start with God's self-revelation to the world and God's invitation to humans to participate in it.[27] Mission starts in the trinitarian activity of God; the Father sends the Son into the world through the enlivening power of the Spirit. The church is brought into God's mission so that, as the Father sent the Son, so too the Son sends the church into the world in the life-giving power of the Spirit to participate in God's redemptive activity. All other mission activity stems from the *missio*

---

26. Ibid.
27. Bosch, *Transforming Mission*, 228.

Dei. Bosch's six postmodern paradigms of mission include mission as evangelism, mission as justice, mission as contextualization and inculturation, mission as liberation, mission as ecumenical and interfaith dialogue, and mission as eschatological hope in action. Fundamentally, he argues that "To participate in mission is to participate in the movement of God's love toward people, since God is the fountain of sending love."[28] We propose the additional category of "mission as renewal" to highlight the charismatic emphasis on love and the kingdom of God.

Bevans and Schroeder have elaborated on Bosch's work and propose four paradigms of mission. These include mission as participation in the *imago Dei*, mission as liberating service to the reign of God, mission as proclamation, and mission as prophetic dialogue. Mission as prophetic dialogue includes components such as witness and proclamation, liturgy, prayer and contemplation, justice, peace, the integrity of creation, and reconciliation. Of note is the role of the life of prayer and contemplation as a missional act for crossing boundaries. Through prayer, Christians align themselves with the purposes of God for the world. Through prayer, people are transformed to be co-workers with God. Through contemplation, people develop a deeper level of attention to the divine that leads into service to the world. This service involves help for the homeless, marginalized, and oppressed, respect and understanding for other cultures and religions, and advocating for political and social justice. Prayer is action in the sense that through prayer people are in touch with God's will for the world as well as the needs and cares of the church and humanity. Prayer and contemplation are embodied practices because they take place in particular social contexts with a definite focus. Prayer can be spontaneous, joyful, and even ecstatic as is commonplace in Pentecostalism. "In sum, liturgy, prayer, and contemplation are powerful ways for Christians to participate in God's mission within God's creation 'as we wait in joyful hope for the coming of our Lord, Jesus Christ.'"[29]

In *Flame of Love*, Clark Pinnock makes some initial proposals regarding the relationship between charismatic renewal and mission. He argues that the Spirit is charismatically present in the church for the sake of mission. The charismatic "miracles and healings of Jesus were not incidental to his mission but concrete evidences of God's reign of love."[30] The transfer-

---

28. Ibid., 390.
29. Bevans and Schroeder, *Constants in Context*, 367–68.
30. Pinnock, *Flame of Love*, 132.

ence of the Spirit from Jesus to the disciples that occurred on the day of Pentecost means that the disciples were empowered to carry out Jesus' mission with the same charismatic authority in order for love to reign. Thus the *charismata* of bearing witness, healing, praising God, miracles, dreams, and visions are described as impulses of power from the Spirit "to transform and commission disciples to become instruments of mission."[31] Whether in terms of healing, visions, or other charismatic gifts, God is free to grant or not to grant their gifting, to offer them to a few or many, to make them mundane or spectacular according to God's sovereign will, although, when granted, all charismatic gifts point to the coming kingdom. They do not, however, replace the need for complete renewal. In other words, charismatic renewal is a gift that points to the renewal of creation.[32]

Pinnock then discusses the relationship between renewal and mission that begins with the personal transformation of the individual, leading to service in the kingdom so that the world may be transformed. Mission is not, according to Pinnock, a human effort in response to a commandment, nor is it obedience to the Great Commission, but is God's spontaneous work to gather and bring justice to the world. The responsibility of Christians is to place themselves at the Spirit's disposal. The Spirit works to renew life and create community for the benefit of human beings. "The Spirit becomes tangible in the deeds of love that function like sacraments in the world," according to Pinnock.[33] This is a holistic mission. Loving one's neighbor also necessitates caring for their needs.[34]

Based on our investigations of the charismatic renewal, we propose that charismatic renewal as mission assists in understanding the role of mission in Pentecostal-Charismatic Christianity. Furthermore, charismatic renewal as mission has the potential to contribute to the theological discussions of mission and the church. For evangelicals, the Great Commission is primary in the *evangelicum* of the church and is understood in the interplay between Word and Deed, which is the proclamation of the gospel and the social action that works towards the image of the kingdom of God. Ministerial vocation and lay engagement in mission are seen as service to the Great Commission in that it is one's Christian duty to preach the gospel to others and to act in ways that are conducive to Christian ideals. Thus,

31. Ibid., 136.
32. Ibid.
33. Ibid., 143.
34. Ibid., 144–45.

evangelicals are on the whole engaged in witness, evangelism, teaching, and missionary endeavors in other cultural contexts as their social action reflects their understanding of the call to missions. Current discussions in missional ecclesiology with theologians such as Lesslie Newbigin, Craig Van Gelder, Darrell L. Guder, and George Hunsberger insist that the particularized context of North America is also a field for missional encounter and cross-cultural engagement.[35]

Although charismatics also place great stress on mission, they believe that working for the Great Commission out of a sense of obedience or duty is a form of works righteousness. This is called "performance." The sin of performance has insidiously perverted the joy and delight of working as co-laborers for the kingdom of God; it produces anxiety in people. It is an egoistic attempt to take control of the work of mission, rather than allowing God to direct the outworking of the kingdom. Co-laboring in the work of the Great Commission is not a performance or duty, but a passion for sharing God's love with others because charismatics have experienced this love for themselves. This mission is exciting, adventurous, and inspires others to engage in the work of ministry as well. For charismatics, the Great Commission is important but it flows out of the commandment of love. The Great Commandment begins with the double action of loving God with all your heart, mind, soul, and strength, and loving your neighbor as yourself. Loving God also has a reciprocal sense in that charismatics believe their love for God is a response to the intimate experience of God loving them. In soaking prayer, charismatics rest in the presence of God's intimate love, replenishing this love energy, and through the experience of prayer are able to expend this energy in care-love. Divine presence is relational, evidenced by the charismatic manifestations experienced in worship and prayer. These manifestations are interpreted as signs of divine love.

The emphasis on relationality, reciprocity, mutuality, inter-subjectivity, and interaction is characteristic of the charismatic renewal.[36] The mutuality and inter-subjectivity of human relationships with one another that are defined by the experience of love are reflective of the relational intimacy that charismatics experience in worship and prayer. These points of emphasis

---

35. See Newbigin's books, *Open Secret*; *Foolishness to the Greeks*; *Gospel in a Pluralist Society*; Gruder, *Missional Church*; Van Gelder, *Essence of the Church*; Hunsberger and Van Gelder, *Church between Gospel and Culture*.

36. Versteeg, *Dutch Pentecostal Church*. The author makes a similar argument from his research of a Vineyard church in the Netherlands, though the component of soaking prayer is missing, suggesting that soaking prayer is an innovation of CTF.

Soaking Prayer and the Advancement of the Kingdom of Love

reflect broader cultural and theological shifts in the Christian relationship to others and to the world.

Pentecostal theologian Frank Macchia has argued that a major theological shift has occurred in understanding the nature of God and that this reflects broader cultural shifts.[37] Macchia maintains that in classical theism God was understood in abstract philosophical categories as an isolated ego acting unilaterally. The emphasis in classical theism was on the timelessness, immovability, and impassibility of God so that God was viewed as the Unmoved Mover.[38] In the twentieth century, however, a shift occurred that understands God in terms of relationship. Now God is viewed more often as personal and relational, but these descriptions appear to be incompatible with the God of classical theism.

According to Macchia, three theological trends have attempted to flesh out the relationality of God: The first is process theology, as defined by Charles Hartshorne.[39] It founds the experience of God on the experiences of the natural world. Second, new avenues in trinitarian theology have opened up that focus on the relationality of the divine persons in the triune life. The triune life becomes normative for how human relationality in community should operate. In this approach, the unity of God is seen as mutual dependence of indwelling. God's love flows from infinite and personal relationality because God is differentiated unity in community.[40] Third, the eschatological view of God, as defined by Jürgen Moltmann and Kazoh Kitamori, proposes that eschatological hope in God's future glory is fundamental for defining a dynamic and relational God.[41] In this view, the power and lure of divine love invites people into relationship, but this love also includes divine suffering because love involves risk and vulnerability. God's suffering was not of necessity, but a free sovereign choice to love a sinful humanity. The cross is the point of the greatest expression of divine love and the point of divine brokenness and suffering.

The charismatic renewal reflects this relational shift, especially in terms of the last two trends noted by Macchia. In fact, the emphasis on the

37. Macchia, "God behind 'The Shack.'" We would like to thank Frank Macchia for providing a printed copy of his lecture.

38. See Peters, *God as Trinity*, 31–32; Aquinas, *Summa contra gentiles*, 1:44.2–4 (pp. 170–71).

39. Hartshorne, *Omnipotence and Other Theological Mistakes*, 82.

40. Macchia, "God behind 'The Shack,'" 10–18.

41. Moltmann, *The Trinity and the Kingdom*, 1–20, 48; Kitamori, *Theology of the Pain of God*, 21.

The Globalization of Christianity

Father's love is an intentional attempt to be more Trinitarian than earlier forms of Pentecostalism. God is not viewed as some transcendent abstract entity, but as the heavenly Father who is immanently relational and desires intimacy with those who love him. Charismatic renewal as mission has at its core the outworking of love in which social acts of care and benevolence flow from a genuine experience of divine love and are directed to the lost and brokenhearted. What Peter Versteeg says of the Vineyard is also true of CTF:

> Knowing God intimately, then, means receiving mercy as an individual as well as receiving mercy for others. Within this ritual structure, human closeness signifies the close presence of God. Intimacy with God, then, is the Vineyard picture of authentic relationship, and as such it reflects the authentic relationship between human beings. It is the desire to have relationships that are voluntary and merciful, outside the laws of achievement, obligation, and reciprocity that permeated everyday human interaction.[42]

Other forms of mission such as evangelism, liberation, justice, active hope, and so on, are not excluded in charismatic renewal as mission, but flow from God's love experienced in personal relationship. Charismatics engage in the work of mission because they want to share the overabundance of love with others in the world. Charismatics have compassion for others because God has shown compassion to them. This compassion is not merely rhetoric but is experienced through inner healing, and signs and wonders that are perceived to be the very presence of the Father in the coming of the kingdom of heaven. Charismatic renewal as mission is the mission of love through which the world will experience the fullness of divine love.

Conclusion

Advancing the kingdom is CTF's program for teaching participants how to live out the Great Commission. "The kingdom of heaven is at hand," as Arnott is fond of saying, meaning that it is about to manifest itself in charismatic wonder but with long-term effects as people carry the kingdom with them into the world. However, the Great Commandment is CTF's vision and priority for experiencing the kingdom where the overwhelming presence of unlimited love inspires participants to love others through a range

42. Versteeg, *Dutch Pentecostal Church*, 145.

Soaking Prayer and the Advancement of the Kingdom of Love

of benevolent activity. Participants claim that through soaking prayer they experience a greater sense of intimacy, relationality, and mutuality with the divine that helps them develop healthier and more intimate relationships with others around them. In other words, charismatics are encouraged to experience the overwhelming love of the Father before they engage in mission. Charismatic renewal as mission is the mission of CTF. We propose that this sense of mission contributes to Bosch's postmodern repertoire of mission. Specifically, charismatic renewal as mission is fundamental to CTF's vision for experiencing the Father's love and giving it away to the rest of the world.

Bibliography

Arnott, John. "God's Call to Go with Jesus." Seminar, Advancing the Kingdom School, Vancouver, n.d.

———. "Opening Message." Catch the Fire Conference, Founders Inn, Virginia Beach: February 2011. Cited from notes taken by the author.

Aquinas, Thomas. *Summa contra gentiles*. Book 1, God. Translated with notes and introduction by Anton C. Pegis. Notre Dame: University of Notre Dame Press, 1955.

Bevans, Stephen B., and Roger P. Schroeder. *Constants in Context: A Theology of Mission for Today*. Maryknoll, NY: Orbis, 2004.

Bosch, David J. *Transforming Mission: Paradigm Shifts in Theology of Mission*. Maryknoll, NY: Orbis, 1991.

Charmaz, Kathy. *Constructing Grounded Theory: A Practical Guide through Qualitative Analysis*. Los Angeles: Sage, 2006.

Collins, Randall. *Interaction Ritual Chains*. Princeton: Princeton University Press, 2004.

Glaser, Barney G., and Anselm L. Straus. *The Discovery of Grounded Theory*. Chicago: Aldine, 1967.

Guder, Darrell L., ed. *Missional Church: A Vision for the Sending of the Church in North America*. Grand Rapids: Eerdmans, 1998.

Hartshorne, Charles. *Omnipotence and Other Theological Mistakes*. Albany: State University of New York, 1984.

Hunsberger, George R., and Craig Van Gelder, eds. *The Church between Gospel and Culture: The Emerging Mission in North America*. Grand Rapids: Eerdmans, 1996.

Johnson, Rolf M. *Three Faces of Love*. DeKalb, IL: Northern Illinois University Press, 2001.

Kitamori, Kazoh. *Theology of the Pain of God*. Richmond: John Knox, 1965.

Lee, Matthew T., and Margaret M. Poloma. *A Sociological Study of the Great Commandment in Pentecostalism: The Practice of Godly Love as Benevolent Service*. Lewiston, NY: Edwin Mellen, 2009.

Lee, Matthew T., Margaret M. Poloma, and Stephen G. Post, "Introduction." In *The Science and Theology of Godly Love*, edited by Matthew T. Lee and Amos Yong, 3–14. DeKalb, IL: Northern Illinois University Press. 2012.

Macchia, Frank. "The God behind 'The Shack': Recent Revolutions in the Theology of God." Public Lecture, Calvin College, Grand Rapids, July 2009.
Moltmann, Jürgen. *The Trinity and the Kingdom*. San Francisco: Harper & Row, 1981.
Newbigin, Lesslie. *Foolishness to the Greeks: The Gospel and Western Culture*. Grand Rapids: Eerdmans, 1986.
———. *The Gospel in a Pluralist Society*. Grand Rapids: Eerdmans, 1989.
———. *The Open Secret: An Introduction to the Theology of Mission*. Rev. ed. Grand Rapids: Eerdmans, 1995.
Peters, Ted. *God as Trinity: Relationality and Temporality in Divine Life*. Minneapolis: Westminster John Knox, 1993.
Pinnock, Clark. *The Flame of Love*. Downers Grove, IL: InterVarsity, 1996.
Poloma, Margaret M. *Main Street Mystics: The Toronto Blessing and Reviving Pentecostalism*. Walnut Creek, CA: Alta Mira, 2003.
Poloma, Margaret M., and John Green. *The Assemblies of God: Godly Love and the Revitalization of American Pentecostalism*. New York: New York University Press, 2010.
Sorokin, Pitirim A. *The Ways and Power of Love*. Philadelphia: Templeton Foundation Press, 2002.
Van Gelder, Craig. *The Essence of the Church: A Community Created by the Spirit*. Grand Rapids: Baker, 2000.
Versteeg, Peter. *The Ethnography of a Dutch Pentecostal Church: Vineyard Utrecht and the International Charismatic Movement*. Lewiston, NY: Edwin Mellen, 2010.
Wilkinson, Michael, and Peter Althouse. *Catch the Fire: Soaking Prayer and Charismatic Renewal*. DeKalb, IL: Northern Illinois University Press, 2014.

7

"Thor and Allah . . . in a hideous, unholy confederacy"
The Armenian Genocide in the Canadian Protestant Press

GORDON L. HEATH

TWENTIETH-CENTURY HISTORY WAS MARRED by devilishly violent acts, some of the most horrendous being the numerous genocides in Europe, Africa, and Asia that led to over one hundred million deaths.[1] The first program of modern times to have the dubious distinction of being recognized as genocide was carried out by the Ottoman Empire (modern-day Turkey).[2] During the First World War, the Turkish government aggressively pursued a policy of genocide against the Armenians within its borders. Estimates of the disaster usually range between one million and one and a half million deaths.[3] Some have even made a connection between the Armenian geno-

1. Graber, *Caravans to Oblivion*, 175.

2. Kiernan claims that the German treatment of the Herero and Nama peoples of South West Africa in 1904 was the first genocide of the century. See Kiernan, "Twentieth Century Genocides," 29. See also Olusoga and Erichsen, *The Kaiser's Holocaust*.

3. Turkish authorities admit 800,000 deaths occurred (not counting tens of thousands of conscripts executed by the military), but not through genocide. See Dadrian, *History of the Armenian Genocide*, 225. Other estimates are higher. For instance, of the 1,500,000 to 2,000,000 pre-war Armenians, 250,000 escaped to Russia. "Of the remaining 1,600,000 about 1,000,000 were killed, half of whom were women and children. Of the surviving 600,000 about 200,000 were forcibly Islamized; and the wretched remnant of 400,000 was found, starving and in rags, by the Allies . . . at the end of the war"

The Globalization of Christianity

cide and the horrors of the Nazi concentration camps: Hitler knew about the fate of the Armenians, and when addressing his generals regarding the harsh treatment of the Reich's enemies, said, "Who, after all, speaks today of the annihilation of the Armenians?"[4]

The response to the atrocities by Canada's closest allies—Britain,[5] America,[6] and France[7]—has had scholarly attention, as has the coverage of secular papers and media.[8] However, there is need for an analysis of genocide in Canadian religious papers to add to the burgeoning literature on the events of 1915–1919.[9] Research on this topic also contributes to the study of the Canadian churches and the First World War, a subject not yet sufficiently developed in Canadian historiography.[10]

Studies of Canadian churches and their reactions to early-twentieth-century genocide deal solely with the Jewish holocaust of the Second World War,[11] as if the Armenian events had not occurred. What was the response

---

(Walker, *Armenia*, 230). Kuper, "Turkish Genocide of Armenians," 52, claims 1,000,000 died. Shirinian, *Quest for Closure*, 33, claims that between 1,200,000 and 1,800,000 died. To be added to these figures are approximately 250,000 Assyro-Chaldeans of the Church of the East lost in battle or massacred. See Guant, *Massacres, Resistance, Protectors*, 300.

4. Bardakjian, *Hitler and the Armenian Genocide*, 1. See also Dadrian, *History of the Armenian Genocide*, ch. 23, and Dekmejian, "Determinants of Genocide." Of course, whether or not there is a causal connection between the two genocides does not change the fact that both were heinous crimes against humanity.

5. Nassibian, *Armenian Question*; Kirakossian, *British Diplomacy*.

6. Peterson, *America and the Armenian Genocide*; Winter, *America and the Armenian Genocide*; Davis, *Slaughterhouse Province*; Balakian, *Burning Tigris*; Payaslian, "United States Response"; Moranian, "Legacy of Paradox."

7. Videlier, "French Society."

8. Kloian, *Armenian Genocide*; Armenian National Committee, *Reported in the Australian Press*; Armenian Youth Federation of Canada, *Genocide in the Canadian Press*; Dobkin, "What Genocide?"; Arissian, "Genocide in the Syrian Press." For media accounts of earlier massacres, see Kirakossian, *British Media Testimony*; Kirakossian, *U.S. Media Testimony*.

9. For a study of Canada's response to the Armenian Genocide, see Shirinian, *Quest for Closure*. For other treatments of the genocide, see Bloxham, *Game of Genocide*; Akcam, *From Empire to Republic*; Graber, *Caravans to Oblivion*; Dadrian, *History of the Armenian Genocide*; Hovannisian, *Remembrance and Denial*; Hovannisian, *Cultural and Ethical Legacies*; Hovannisian, *Genocide in Perspective*; Hovannisian, *Looking Backward, Moving Forward*.

10. For a discussion of published material on Canadian churches and the war, see Heath, "Canadian Churches and War." See also Heath, *Canadian Churches and the First World War*.

11. Abella and Troper, *None Is Too Many*, claim that Canadian churches were silent

of the churches to the genocide that occurred more than two decades before the horrors of Nazi Germany? Unlike the genocide of the Second World War, events in Turkey were well known in the West almost from the onset of violence: "From a comparative perspective, the remarkable feature of the Turkish genocide of Armenians was its immediate documentation by the accounts of eyewitnesses and of contemporary analysts."[12]

By the end of the nineteenth century and into the twentieth, the Protestant churches had an influence on English-Canadian society unlike that of any other institution, and they sought to use it to forge a distinctly Christian nation.[13] Through their wartime services, sermons, organizations, and literature, the churches desired not only to bolster the faith of their adherents but also to shape political convictions and mobilize their constituents. One way in which they did so was through their publications,[14] and the Armenian genocide was one of the issues that the Canadian Protestant press addressed.[15] This chapter demonstrates that the genocide was well-

---

regarding the plight of the Jews in Nazi Europe. Reacting to this claim, Davies and Nefsky state that the answer to the question "were they silent?" is both yes and no. They find examples of church leaders, governing bodies, and leaders in the pulpit decrying their plight, but also note that there was no sustained outcry from the leaders or rank-and-file members. Genizi argues that while the churches did critique the Nazi treatment of Jews, the deeply rooted anti-Semitism within the churches muted the reaction, and also led churches to be unfairly critical of the new nation of Israel. See Abella and Troper, *None Is Too Many*; Nefsky, *How Silent Were the Churches?*; Nefsky, "Church of England in Canada"; Nefsky, "United Church"; Genizi, *Canadian Protestant Churches*. See also Shantz, "Kingston Christians." For commentary on the genocide in Rwanda, see Bowler, "We Wish to Inform You."

12. Kuper, "Turkish Genocide of Armenians," 45.

13. The Anglicans, Baptists, Methodists, and Presbyterians were the largest and most influential Protestant churches at that time, and unless noted otherwise, "churches" refers to these four denominations. In 1911, there were 1,079,000 Methodists, 1,115,000 Presbyterians, 1,043,000 Anglicans, and 382,000 Baptists for a total of 50.6 percent of the Canadian population. In the same year, there were 2,833,000 Catholics, for a total of 39.3 percent of the Canadian population. The other 10 percent were smaller, mainly Protestant, groups and members of other non-Christian religions. For statistics, see Semple, *The Lord's Dominion*, 182.

14. For the role of the Protestant press and the shaping of political opinions, see Heath, "Forming Sound Public Opinion."

15. The publications examined in this chapter are as follows: *Canadian Churchman, Montreal Churchman, Maritime Baptist, Canadian Baptist, Christian Guardian, Presbyterian Record, Presbyterian Witness, The Presbyterian, The Westminster, Presbyterian and Westminster, Queen's Quarterly, Diocesan Gazette, Mission World*, and *The Missionary Outlook*. I would like to thank the Social Science Humanities Research Council for financial assistance for archival visits.

documented in the religious press, and argues that the genocide provided the churches with a powerful moral justification for maintaining that the war needed to be fought to a victorious conclusion. The message conveyed in the Protestant press was that Armenian suffering would only end with a military victory over Germany and its Turkish ally. "Thor and Allah" were considered to be in a "hideous and unholy confederacy," and the war was being waged to put an end to the horrors wrought upon the world by that alliance. The chapter conclusion will briefly address the question of whether the churches did enough in response to the Armenian genocide.

The extent and nature of the coverage varied in the denominational press. The prestigious bi-monthly, Presbyterian *Queen's Quarterly*, published one extensive article on the massacres. The Methodist missionary-focused *Missionary Outlook* referred to the disaster at least eight times, but only in a cursory way and only as it related to mission work, for its focus was on the Methodist Church work in China, Japan, India, and Canada. Various monthly diocesan papers made little mention of the genocide, partly because their focus was news as it related to the work of the diocese. The weekly papers that sought to act as newspapers, such as the *Christian Guardian*, *Canadian Churchman*, or *Presbyterian Witness*, included more frequent updates and analyses from an eclectic mix of sources. Nevertheless, these papers often went months without mentioning the plight of Armenians because Canadian readers were primarily interested in the conflagration on the Western Front (where the Canadian Expeditionary Force served) and the submarine-infested Atlantic, not to mention the business of their denomination.

THE FACT OF THE ARMENIAN GENOCIDE

The term "genocide" was invented in the 1940s by Raphael Lemkin to describe the Turkish handling of Armenians and the Nazi treatment of the Jews. The word is made from the Greek *genos* (people or nation) and the Latin suffix–*cide* (murder).[16] The United Nations adopted the term on 9 December 1948 in the Convention on the Prevention and Punishment of the Crime of Genocide, often referred to as the Genocide Convention. The Convention defines genocide as "the intent to destroy, in whole or in part, a national, ethnic, racial or religious group."[17] It is more than deaths

16. Weitz, *Century of Genocide*, 8.
17. Millennium Assembly of the United Nations, "Convention on the Prevention and

as a consequence of war or localized pogroms; rather, it is a systematic and concerted attempt to wipe out a people. Genocide is a controversial and contested term, but it serves the important purpose of describing an attempt to eliminate a particular people.

Based on this definition, can what happened to the Armenians be deemed "genocide"? Despite intense political pressure from the Turkish government, a growing number of nations—including Canada (2004)—have declared that the violence perpetrated against Armenians was indeed genocide.[18] While it is beyond the scope of this chapter to defend this view, I agree with it, and with Philip Jenkins, who states, "If the word *genocide* has any meaning whatever, it certainly applies" to the treatment of Armenians and other Christian minorities under Ottoman rule during those years.[19] A great deal of primary source material has been gathered on the Armenian genocide, with a well-developed historiography.[20] Nevertheless, the interpretation of these sources is contested, with some denying that genocide even occurred.[21] There is a professional and moral responsibility for historians to use academic freedom properly, but that is not always the case with deniers of the Armenian genocide, especially among Turkish historians.[22] There are "striking similarities" in the methodologies and objectives of Armenian Genocide and Jewish Holocaust deniers, and denying the events is cause for alarm, for in the denial of the past the "process of annihilation is thus advanced and completed."[23]

Punishment of the Crime of Genocide."

18. For the Canadian statement, see Armenian National Institute, "Canadian House of Commons Resolution," which resolved: "That This House Acknowledge the Armenian Genocide of 1915 and Condemn This Act as a Crime against Humanity." For Turkish reaction, see CBC News, "Turkey Condemns Canada's Armenian Genocide Vote."

19. Jenkins, *Lost History*, 162.

20. For instance, see Sarafian, "Archival Trail." See also Barton, *Turkish Atrocities*; Miller, *Survivors*; Davis, *Slaughterhouse Province*. For historiographical issues, see Miller, "Oral History Perspective"; Miller and Touryan, "Armenian Survivors"; Hovannisian, "Bitter-Sweet Memories"; Shirinian, "Survivor Memoirs"; Peroomian, "Problematic Aspects."

21. For instance, see Oke, *Armenian Question*; Lewy, *Disputed Genocide*.

22. See Ternon, "Freedom and Responsibility"; Smith et al., "Professional Ethics"; Nichanian, "Truth of the Facts"; Hovannisian, "Patterns of Denial"; Guroian, "Collective Responsibility"; Theriault, "Denial and Free Speech."

23. Hovannisian, "Denial of the Armenian Genocide," 201–202.

The Globalization of Christianity

The Canadian Protestant Press and the Genocide

The closing decades of the nineteenth century saw the rapid decline of the Ottoman Empire and its retreat from the Balkans. Once a mighty empire that had threatened central Europe, the Ottoman Empire had devolved into the "sick man" of Europe. As long as the Empire had been expanding, minorities (of which there were many) had usually lived in relative safety. However, as Niall Ferguson notes, "The worst time to live under imperial rule is when that rule is crumbling."[24] Ottoman decline meant that minorities such as the Armenians faced new uncertainties, danger, and persecution.[25] The reports in the Anglican *Canadian Church Magazine and Mission News* in 1896 provide a glimpse into the travails of the Christian Armenians in the Ottoman Empire in the late–nineteenth century:

> The unfortunate Armenians, being still slaughtered right and left, must wonder why among the millions of Christian people throughout the world no one steps in to help them. The sword of the Kurd is still bloody; the Sultan of Turkey knows no pity; Mohammedans still mow Christians down, and Christian powers seem not to care. Some great result, at present unforeseen, may follow from these horrors, but ordinary people cannot help wondering why the Christian world allows them to continue.[26]

The Hamidian Massacres (1894–1896) that led to 100,000 to 300,000 deaths, to which this report was referring, were only a prelude to subsequent horrors. In the final decades of the nineteenth century, the foreign policy of Britain was to prop up the Ottoman Empire so that it acted as a bulwark against Russian expansion, which was deemed a threat to Britain's connection to India. Article 61 of the Congress of Berlin (1878) stipulated that the Ottoman government treat its Armenian subjects justly, or the Western powers would intervene. The British attempted to respond militarily to the massacres in 1895–1896, but opposition, primarily from Russia, meant that it did not; this inaction of the Great Powers and their failure to respond "certainly encouraged" the Ottomans to continue in their mistreatment

---

24. Ferguson, *War of the World*, 176.

25. Hovannisian, "Historical Dimensions," 20.

26. "Editorial Notes," *Canadian Church Magazine and Mission News*, February 1896, 43. See also "Editorial Notes," *Canadian Church Magazine and Mission News*, January 1896, 19. For a late-Victorian response to the Turkish treatment of Armenians, see Hopkins, *Sword of Islam*.

"Thor and Allah . . . in a hideous, unholy confederacy"

of the Armenians.[27] Consequently, further massacres followed in Tokat (1897), Sasun and Spaghank (1900), Diarbekir (1900), Mush and Sasun (1901), Bitlis and Van (1902), and Adana (1909).

In July 1908 a coup led by military officers replaced the Sultan. These "Young Turks" and their political organization, Committee of Union and Progress (CUP), sought to reverse imperial decline and to rejuvenate the Empire through reforms and modernization under the banner, "Liberty, equality, and fraternity."[28] The hope for minorities such as the Armenians was that the massacres and mistreatment of the past would end with the policies of the new government. However, that was not to be, for ideology, events, politics, and hatred conspired against them.

The ideology of the Young Turks was a pan-Turkanism that replaced a multi-ethnic heterogeneous Ottoman Empire with a homogenous Turkish state of one nation, one people.[29] Various minorities in the Balkans, such as the Greeks or Bulgarians, had been able to throw off the yoke of Turkish rule, often with Western or Russian intervention on their behalf.[30] The aim for the new government was to make this impossible in Anatolian Turkey, and thus there was a pressing need to get rid of minorities, the largest by far being the approximately 1,800,000 Armenians. The outbreak of war in 1914 provided cover and a pretext for elimination of the Armenians who lived within the Empire's borders. The fear of Armenians allying with the Entente Powers, especially the Russian Empire, which had a significant Armenian population along the border with the Ottoman Empire, was a part of Young Turk concern.[31]

The Armenian Genocide started in April 1915. The methods of eliminating the Armenians were arrests, executions, and deportations. Deportation merely "served as a cloak for massacre."[32] Usually males were arrested first, and then taken away and executed en masse. Women, children, and the elderly were then rounded up under the pretext of being "relocated."

---

27. Somakian, *Empires in Conflict*, 27.

28. Ibid., 37.

29. Hovannisian, "Historical Dimensions," 27–28; Akcam, *From Empire to Republic*, chs. 3–4; Somakian, *Empires in Conflict*, ch. 4.

30. Dadrian, *History of the Armenian Genocide*, chs. 2–3, 6.

31. Deniers of the Armenian genocide often justify the Ottoman government's conduct by pointing to the internal threat and provocation of Armenians. See Melson, "Provocation or Nationalism"; Somakian, *Empires in Conflict*, 82–85.

32. Kuper, "Turkish Genocide of Armenians," 49.

Deportation itself was a deadly nightmare, as the following eyewitness account indicates:

> Children cried themselves to death, men threw themselves to their death on the rocks while women threw their own children into wells and pregnant mothers leapt singing into the Euphrates. They died all the deaths of the world, the deaths of all the centuries. I saw men gone mad, feeding on their own excrement, women cooking their newborn children . . . People lay apathetically among the heaps of dead and emaciated bodies, waiting for death . . . Yet all this is still only a fraction of what I saw with my own eyes or was related to me by friends or travelers, or by the outcasts themselves.[33]

Among the horrors of the "caravans to oblivion"[34] was the mass "sexual violence and gender-specific persecution of victims [usually female],"[35] the Islamization of children taken from Armenian parents,[36] the theft of property and land (never to be returned), the desecration and destruction of churches and holy places, and the extension of genocide to the Assyrian Christians in the Middle East (Syria).[37] The large-scale deportations of the Armenians continued into 1916, but "massacres, deportations and persecutions" continued even in the years immediately following the war and while the Allies deliberated over peace terms.[38]

Canadian newspapers such as the *Montreal Star*, *Globe* (Toronto), *Daily Telegraph* (Berlin = Kitchener, Ontario), *Manitoba Free Press*, *Ottawa*

---

33. Hofmann, "German Eyewitness Reports," 66.
34. See Graber, *Caravans to Oblivion*.
35. Derderian, "Common Fate," 1.
36. Marashlian, "Finishing the Genocide," 121.

37. David Guant's summary and analysis is a sober description of the massacres of Christians in eastern Turkey and further east and south into modern-day Syria, Iraq, and Iran during the First World War, including communities such as the Syriac Orthodox, the Assyrian Church, the Chaldean Church, the Syriac Catholic Church, Armenian Apostolic Church, and Armenian Catholic Church (as well a small number of Protestant missionaries and converts). See Guant, *Massacres, Resistance, Protectors*. See also Khosroeva, "Assyrian Genocide."

38. By passing a law that stated that all properties of non-Muslims vacated before the Treaty of Lausanne (July 1923) were to pass to the Turkish government, the founders of the "Republic of Turkey finished the Armenian Genocide, by plundering and eliminating the remnants of the Ottoman Armenians, who otherwise might have reclaimed their confiscated property as citizens of the new republic" (Marashlian, "Finishing the Genocide," 138).

"Thor and Allah . . . in a hideous, unholy confederacy"

Evening Journal, La Patrie (Montreal), and *Vancouver Daily* reported on the disaster unfolding in the Ottoman Empire.[39] Protestant denominational papers also published reports, and the following is a summary and analysis of that coverage.

An article in the *Presbyterian Witness*, noting the massacres of Christians in Persia, indicates that reporting in the denominational press of Turkish atrocities began at least as early as April 1915.[40] More extensive coverage in the denominational press began in October 1915. The *Maritime Baptist* reporting is indicative of the type of initial commentary: estimates of 500,000 deaths and details of the sufferings of Armenians.[41] A month later its Ontario counterpart, the *Canadian Baptist*, estimated that 800,000 had died, and more were dying gruesome deaths at the hands of the Turkish government:

> The massacre that is going on now is said to aim at the complete extermination of the whole Armenian race. It is estimated that already 800,000 have been slaughtered in cold blood . . . This wholesale slaughter is accompanied by the most fiendish and revolting acts of cruelty known to humanity. In Trepizond 10,000 Armenians were forced into boats, taken out to sea and drowned. Multitudes have been compelled to leave their homes and have been driven in caravans into the deserts, with robber bands, by prearrangement, falling upon them, here and there by the way; while those escaping death at the hands of these are left to perish on the sandy wastes . . . The saddest part of the whole dreadful business is that these massacres are deliberately planned and carried out by the Turkish Government, the ally of Germany.[42]

The *Canadian Churchman* echoed these sentiments in its initial reporting, concluding that the "atrocities visited upon the Armenians came from the Turkish Capital as a part of a regular program."[43]

39. For a brief summary of newspaper reporting in Canada, see Armenian Youth Federation of Canada, *Genocide in the Canadian Press*; Shirinian, *Quest for Closure*, 61–75.

40. "Massacres of Christians in Persia," *Presbyterian Witness*, 3 April 1915, 1.

41. "Unhappy Armenia," *Maritime Baptist*, 6 October 1915, 1.

42. "The Armenian Massacres," *Canadian Baptist*, 11 November 1915, 4.

43. "Armenia," *Canadian Churchman*, 28 October 1915, 679. For other examples of initial reporting, see "Turkey and Armenia," *Canadian Churchman*, 14 October 1915, 647–48; "The Murder of a Nation," *Canadian Churchman*, 16 December 1915, 803; "Fighting the Turk," *Christian Guardian*, 1 September 1915, 4; "The Murdering Turk," *Christian Guardian*, 6 October 1915, 4; "The Armenian Atrocities," *Christian Guardian*,

While Protestants in Canada had reservations about Eastern European Christians immigrating to Canada, the denominational press reflected none of those prejudices when it came to commenting about the Armenians suffering under Turkish rule. Protestant papers looked upon Armenians as an "ancient Christian people" and a "Christian nation." If any doubted their sincerity, their martyrdom proved that Armenian Christianity was genuine: "The Armenians are Christians, using that term in its usual wide significance. That their religion, however imperfect, must be a great reality to them, [is] seen from the multitudes of them that have chosen martyrdom rather than deny Christ."[44] A comparison was made between the faithfulness of early Christians under the persecution of the Romans and Armenians under harsh Turkish rule.[45] The Church Father Tertullian's well-known adage, "the blood of the martyrs is the seed of the church," was also invoked with the hope that Armenian martyrdoms would lead to the conversion of Muslims.[46]

Attempts to raise money in Canada for Armenian relief were widespread, and the denominational papers do provide glimpses of church support. In 1916, S. H. Sarkissian, a native of Armenia and a Presbyterian minister, was invited to speak to the Presbyterian General Assembly in Winnipeg in order to draw attention to the plight of Armenians.[47] A few months later Sarkissian published in *The Presbyterian* an article that decried the "barbarities" of the Armenian atrocities.[48] In that article he also

---

13 October 1915, 4; "The Stricken Armenians," *Christian Guardian*, 10 November 1915, 3–4; "War and Missions in Turkey," *The Missionary Outlook*, September 1915, 197; "Missionary Notes," *The Missionary Outlook*, February 1916, 26; "The Doom of Turkey," *Presbyterian Witness*, 10 April 1915, 1; "The Martyrdom of Armenia," *Presbyterian Witness*, 2 October 1915, 1; "Turkish Atrocities," *Presbyterian Witness*, 16 October 1915, 1; "The Armenian Tragedy," *Presbyterian Witness*, 11 December 1915, 1; "No Relief for Armenia," *Maritime Baptist*, 13 October 1915, 1; "The Armenian Massacres," *Maritime Baptist*, 10 November 1915, 8. While not an example of early reporting, the article in the *Queen's Quarterly* was one of the most detailed descriptions in the denominational press of the atrocities. See L. P. Chambers, "The Armenian Deportations," *Queen's Quarterly*, July-September, 1917, 1–9.

44. "The Armenian Massacres," *Canadian Baptist*, 11 November 1915, 4. See also the same article in the *Maritime Baptist*, 10 November 1915, 8–9.

45. "Lord Bryce on the Armenian Situation," *Presbyterian Witness*, 7 April 1917, 5.

46. "The Blood of the Martyrs," *Presbyterian Record*, July 1917, 204.

47. "Fifteenth Sederunt," 47.

48. S. H. Sarkissian, "The Sorrows of Armenia," *The Presbyterian*, 26 October 1916, 354–55.

"Thor and Allah . . . in a hideous, unholy confederacy"

noted how, in response to his visits and appeals, churches in the Brandon Presbytery gave around $500 for relief. The *Presbyterian and Westminster* promoted the work of the Armenian and Syrian Relief Fund Committee, and encouraged giving to the Sunday School collection planned for 20 January 1918,[49] as did the *Christian Guardian*.[50] The *Canadian Churchman* exhorted its readers to support relief for Armenians:

> One of the saddest of the many sad conditions created by the present war is that of Armenia. A simple, peace-loving, agricultural people have been driven from their homes, slaughtered by thousands, and the remnant left to serve as slaves to their Moslem rulers, or driven into exile . . . May God awaken in this country a keener sense of the opportunities placed within its reach of feeding the starving souls and bodies of those less fortunate in other parts of the world.[51]

The Anglican Primate issued an appeal to church leaders in 1917 and asked that an appeal be made in the various dioceses. The *Canadian Churchman* was asked to cooperate with the appeal, and its response was: "It is scarcely necessary to say that it will be glad to do anything in its power to help on such a worthy cause."[52] Consequently, it supported the Sunday School

---

49. "Armenians and Syrians," *Presbyterian and Westminster*, 27 December 1917, 601. This article states that the Sunday School relief effort was "heartily endorsed" by the Sunday School Boards of the Methodist, Baptist, Anglican, Congregational, and Presbyterian Churches. The Presbyterian *Queen's Quarterly* encouraged support for the Armenian Relief Fund Association of Canada. See L. P. Chambers, "The Armenian Deportations," *Queen's Quarterly*, July-September 1917, 9.

50. "For Relief in Armenia and Syria," *Christian Guardian*, 26 December 1917, 4; "Starving Armenia and Syria," *Christian Guardian*, 16 January 1918, 2.

51. "Armenian Relief," *Canadian Churchman*, 9 November 1916, 711. A Christmas appeal a month later widened the appeal to suffering children throughout Europe and Turkey: "The children of Armenia, Serbia, Poland, Belgium, have died by thousands of exposure, hunger, or violence. And even in other lands such as Germany, France, and one might almost add, Great Britain . . . Let us search out the poor and needy, the fatherless and motherless, the sad and the sorrowing in our midst and let us endeavour by every means in our power to cheer and brighten their lives and to make the Christmas season more nearly what Christ would have it be." See "Children and the War," *Canadian Churchman*, 21 December 1916, 809.

52. "Armenian and Assyrian Relief," *Canadian Churchman*, 24 May 1917, 327. For other examples of support for the Armenians (and Assyrian Christians), see "Armenia," *Canadian Churchman*, 4 November 1915, 704; "Assyrian Christians," *Canadian Churchman*, 30 December 1915, 842; "Armenian and Assyrian Relief," *Canadian Churchman*, 8 November 1917, 713.

collection in 1918, and reported that money donated by Canadian Sunday Schools for the Armenian-Syrian Relief Fund appeal in January 1918 was over $70,000 (over $600,000 was jointly raised by American and Canadian Sunday Schools).[53] Various donations from churches were also noted,[54] and efforts were made to draw attention to Serbian relief.[55] In the aftermath of the war, the diocesan paper *Montreal Churchman* encouraged the diocese to support another special offering for the Armenians.[56]

But how best to stop the atrocities? Very quickly it was concluded that the Turkish government would only respond to military force. Appeals from Western diplomats had fallen on deaf ears, and the only way to end Armenian suffering was a military victory over Germany and its Turkish ally. This fusion of war aims—the defeat of Germany and the ending of atrocities perpetrated against the Armenians—has been overlooked by those who study the rhetoric of the churches and the First World War.

As *A War with a Silver Lining* demonstrates, during the South African War (1899–1902) Canadian English Protestants were imbued with an ardent imperialism, and were with few exceptions firmly and enthusiastically committed to the British Empire and Canada's growing role within it.[57] This imperial support did not lessen in the interim leading up to the First World War; indeed, support for the Empire was one of the reasons for such ardent backing for the war among English Protestants.[58] The churches also believed the war against pan-Germanism was a righteous one that needed

53. "Armenian Relief," *Canadian Churchman*, 14 March 1918, 169; "Sunday Schools and Armenian Relief," *Canadian Churchman*, 21 March 1918, 187.

54. "Armenian and Assyrian Relief," *Canadian Churchman*, 12 July 1917, 443.

55. "For Serbian Relief," *Canadian Churchman*, 7 February 1918, 94; "For Serbian Relief," *Canadian Churchman*, 21 February 1918, 125; "Serbian Culture," *Canadian Churchman*, 28 February 1918, 141; "A Serbian Priest on Faith and War," *Canadian Churchman*, 14 March 1918, 173.

56. "An Aftermath of the War," *Montreal Churchman*, January 1919, 6. For examples of other pleas for assistance, see "Syrian Suffering," *Diocesan Gazette*, August 1917, 10.

57. For analysis of imperialism in the churches, see Heath, *War with a Silver Lining*; Heath, "Deifying Monarchs"; Heath, "Citizens of That Mighty Empire"; Heath, "Sin in the Camp"; Heath, "Passion for Empire." For studies of Canada and Empire, see Berger, *Sense of Power*; Penlington, *Canada and Imperialism*; Page, "Canada and the Imperial Idea"; Page, *Boer War*; Page, "Carl Berger"; Cole, "Canada's 'Nationalistic' Imperialists"; Cook, "George R. Parkin"; Buckner, "Whatever Happened"; Buckner, "Canada." For a study of Canadian anti-imperial sentiment, see Miller, "English-Canadian Opposition"; Ostergaard, "Canadian Nationalism." For French-Canadian views of empire, see Silver, "Quebec Attitudes."

58. For instance, see Angus, "World of the Tiger"; Richards, "Ministry of Propaganda."

to be fought despite the horrific casualties.[59] In the words of an editorial in the *Presbyterian Witness*, there was to be no "truce with hell," meaning the Kaiser and his henchmen who sat "in Satan's seat in Berlin."[60]

In much of the denominational papers' rhetoric there was a fusion of war aims. The war was portrayed as a righteous battle against both the evils of a barbaric Hun that committed unspeakable deeds, and a fiendish Turkish ally who was equally despicable. The *Presbyterian Witness* made it clear that the war was being waged against two equally evil empires:

> Enver Pasha and the Young Turks have slain or enslaved in less than a year 800,000 Christians resident within the Turkish dominions . . . It is this monster of iniquity, that is drenching the earth with human blood and turning whole lands into veritable valleys of weeping, this nation that has turned its destructive power against the fairest and most precious things in life, this Godless, Christless incarnation of evil force, that the more civilized nations of the world have united to restrain and overthrow. Surely if ever there was a holy war, it is that in which our Empire is now engaged in defence of human freedom, and Christian civilization against the barbarous hordes of the German Kaiser and his bloodthirsty Moslem ally.[61]

Another paper printed an article that stated that a victory for the Entente Powers would be a victory for righteousness, whereas a victory for the Central Powers would mean the horrors of "Belgium, Serbia, and Armenia" foisted upon Canada.[62] The inclusion of Armenia in the list of dangers to Canada may have been rhetorical flourish, but its inclusion is significant nonetheless: the war was portrayed as being waged to protect Canada from the threat of an Armenian-style genocide.

The behavior of both Germany and Turkey on the battlefield was considered by the wartime papers to be evidence that the Central Powers were morally bankrupt. The alleged and actual barbarism of the Germans, especially in their advance through Belgium in the opening months of the war, motivated many to enlist. The torpedoing and sinking of ships such as the passenger liner Lusitania further confirmed, in the minds of many,

59. Angus, "World of the Tiger"; Brewer, "Diocese of Antigonish"; Davidson, "Preaching the Great War"; Fowler, "Keeping the Faith"; "MacDonald, "From Just War to Crusade"; Richards, "Ministry of Propaganda."

60. "No Truce with Hell," *Presbyterian Witness*, 21 July 1917, 4.

61. "Universal Service," *Presbyterian Witness*, 6 November 1915, 4.

62. David Williams, "The World Situation," *Canadian Churchman*, 30 May 1918, 344.

the inferiority of German "Kultur" and the righteousness of the Entente Powers' cause. However, it was the conduct of both Germany and Turkey that helped to clarify the issues at stake in the war:

> In moral advantages the year has put us in a position very much more secure than was ours at the beginning of the year. The publication of Viscount Bryce's report as to Belgium, and the facts that have come to light as to Eastern Europe and as to the Armenians have made clear the spirit of our foes, and the sinking of the Lusitania and of other vessels has given an instantaneous photograph of the German attitude that nothing can change . . . The moral issue in the present struggle is so clear that there can be only one result, and the call of duty is so clear that no one must hesitate when the hand of duty points to him.[63]

The war was deemed to be a defense of civilization against barbarism. Canada and the British Empire were at risk of conquest if both Germany and Turkey were not stopped in Europe.

The German and Ottoman Empires were allies, and Germany not only had military and diplomatic personnel in Turkey, but also citizens such as missionaries, doctors, businessmen, and laborers, who were often eyewitnesses of the atrocities. Much has been written about German involvement in the genocide, with one historian claiming that it ranged from "active resistance to complicity."[64] While present-day historians may detect ranges of, and subtleties in, German engagement with the genocide, the wartime papers in Canada did not. The Germans were deemed to be guilty on a number of fronts. First, they could have forced the Turks to end the attacks: "One word from Germany would stop this awful tragedy and save the lives of at least a remnant of this noble race."[65] Yet Germany, at least as portrayed in the papers, did nothing. Second, and even more damning, was the fact that the Turkish government was acting with the "full consent of

---

63. "A Survey of the Year," *Canadian Baptist*, 30 December 1915, 8. For other commentary on the moral issues of the war, see "An Important Declaration," *Diocesan Gazette*, February-March 1917, 26–28.

64. Kaiser, "Baghdad Railway," 95. See also Walker, *Armenia*, 231–36; Bloxham, *Game of Genocide*, ch. 3.

65. J. G. Brown, "The Armenian Massacres," *Canadian Baptist*, 11 November 1915, 4. For similar sentiment, see "Turkey and Armenia," *Canadian Churchman*, 14 October 1915, 647; "Armenia," *Canadian Churchman*, 28 October 1915, 679; "Made in Germany," *Canadian Churchman*, 10 October 1918, 649, 657; "Unhappy Armenia," *Maritime Baptist*, 6 October 1915, 1; "No Relief for Armenia," *Maritime Baptist*, 13 October 1915, 1.

"Thor and Allah . . . in a hideous, unholy confederacy"

Germany, if not at her instigation."⁶⁶ Third, even if Germany had asked the Turkish government to stop the atrocities, the Turks could have pointed to the German treatment of Belgium and Poland as justification for their own actions against the Armenians.⁶⁷ The German's hands were "as deeply dyed in human blood as are those of the Turk."⁶⁸ In all cases, the papers presented a case that implicated Germany in the genocide, and that guilt indicated that the "ideals of the Sultan and the Kaiser in the conduct of this war [were] identical,"⁶⁹ or, in the words of J. Lovell Murray, "Thor and Allah were linked . . . in a hideous, unholy confederacy."⁷⁰

Accounts of atrocities against Armenians served the same purpose as German atrocity stories: they constructed an image of the "other" that supported the war effort and motivated citizens to enlist and soldiers to fight. However, accounts of Armenian atrocities went beyond describing the events to both amplify and confirm an image of the "terrible Turk" that was common in the West.⁷¹ Turks were portrayed as a race without virtue: "In respect of militarism, the Turk above all other peoples on the earth today, seems to have most completely embodied the evil inherent in it, and this, moreover, without having any of the compensating virtues (with the possible exception of courage alone) manifested even in Germany under a military system."⁷²

---

66. "Unhappy Armenia," *Maritime Baptist*, 6 October 1915, 1. See also "Editorial Notes," *Presbyterian Witness*, 3 August 1918, 4; L. P. Chambers, "The Armenian Deportations," *Queen's Quarterly*, July-September, 1917, 8.

67. "The Martyrdom of Armenia," *Presbyterian Witness*, 2 October 1915, 1.

68. "Turkish Atrocities," *Presbyterian Witness*, 16 October 1915, 1.

69. J. G. Brown, "The Armenian Massacres," *Canadian Baptist*, 11 November 1915, 4.

70. J. Lovell Murray, "Islam and the War," *Mission World*, January 1919, 556.

71. "When the unspeakable Turk permitted his evil genius to draw him upon war against the nation to which he owed almost his very existence for the last century or more, there was a general feeling of satisfaction that at last he would be driven bag and baggage out of Europe . . . The recent outrages against the Christians in Persia have shown the Turk up in his old character of barbarian and murderer, and the nations are asking why such people should be permitted any longer to curse any territory of the earth." See "The Doom of Turkey," *Presbyterian Witness*, 10 April 1915, 1. The *Montreal Churchman* spoke of the "barbarous Hun" and the "despicable Turk." See "After Three Years of War," *Montreal Churchman*, August 1917, 1. The *Missionary Outlook* mentioned the "terrible Turk." See "Missionary Notes," *The Missionary Outlook*, July 1918, 146; "Missionary Notes," *The Missionary Outlook*, March 1916, 50.

72. James Endicott, "Ought the Turkish Rule in Europe to Be Ended?" *Christian Guardian*, 24 January 1917, 7.

The "Turks" were an inferior race that exterminated all minorities who were unfortunate enough to live within their borders, incapable of "governing others, and even incapable of governing [themselves]."[73] Turkish rule had a "deadening effect" upon Muslims and Christians since it had made "no single vital contribution" to the "raising of the standard of life" in any marked way; the only Turkish "original contribution" to civilization was the "harem."[74] The end of Turkish rule, consequently, was considered to be a boon to all within and outside Ottoman borders,[75] and, by what was deemed to be God's providence, Turkey had joined with a lost cause that provided the opportunity to end the "murders and persecutions of Christ's people" in Ottoman territory.[76]

The massacres of Armenians led to popular calls in the West for Turkey to be punished, its empire dismembered, and the nation reduced to a small state outside of the boundaries of Europe.[77] These sentiments were echoed in the denominational press, especially in the closing months of the war. In the words of the *Christian Guardian*, Turkey "had absolutely filled to overflowing its cup of iniquity, and ... the day of its rule in the continent of Europe ought to be brought to a close."[78] In reaction to the announcement of the surrender of the Ottomans, the *Maritime Baptist* declared that the time had come "for removing the curse of the Turk from Europe and for breaking his power over other tribes and races. Without exception the rule of the Turk has brought nothing but suffering and destruction in its train."[79] British (or American)

---

73. "The Fate of Turkey," *Canadian Baptist*, 26 December 1918, 1.

74. James Endicott, "Ought the Turkish Rule in Europe to Be Ended?" *Christian Guardian*, 24 January 1917, 7.

75. For other examples of commentary on Turkish rule, see H. U. Weitbrecht, "Turkey and Islam," *Canadian Churchman*, 11 March 1915, 151; Binney S. Black, "Constantinople and Its People," *Westminster*, November 1915, 458; A. S. Morton, "The Changing Map of Europe," *Westminster*, January 1916, 48; Principal Rexford, "Jerusalem Again under the Cross," *Montreal Churchman*, January 1918, 1; "The Holy Land and the War," *Diocesan Gazette*, November 1917, 6–7; "The City of God," *Diocesan Gazette*, February 1918, 11–12; H. D. Ranns, "The Balkan States: A Problem in European Politics," *Christian Guardian*, 13 September 1916, 9–10; "Missionary Notes," *The Missionary Outlook*, July 1918, 146.

76. "The Bishop's Message," *Montreal Churchman*, September 1916, 1.

77. Akcam, *From Empire to Republic*, ch. 6.

78. "The Turkish Situation," *Christian Guardian*, 24 January 1917, 6.

79. "The Surrender of Turkey," *Maritime Baptist*, 6 November 1918, 1. See also James Endicott, "Ought the Turkish Rule in Europe to Be Ended?" *Christian Guardian*, 24 January 1917, 7–8.

> "Thor and Allah ... in a hideous, unholy confederacy"

rule in Mesopotamia where the Ottomans once ruled would lead to a marked improvement in justice,[80] and the end of Turkish "tyranny and cruelty" everywhere would allow for long-misruled peoples to "rejoice and blossom as the rose."[81] The Turk should also never again be allowed to "exercise his corrupt and oppressive misrule over Christian races."[82]

Conclusion

Studies of Canadian churches and their reactions to early twentieth-century genocide deal solely with the Jewish holocaust of the Second World War as if the Armenian events had not occurred. This chapter argues that the Armenian genocide was documented in the press, and that the genocide provided powerful moral justification for why the war needed to be fought to a victorious conclusion. The churches believed that the Armenian suffering would only end through a military victory over Germany and its Turkish ally. "Thor and Allah" were considered to be in a "hideous and unholy confederacy," and the war was being waged to put an end to the horrors wrought upon the world by that alliance. There was a fusion of war aims—the defeat of Germany and the ending of atrocities perpetrated against the Armenians.

The question "Did the churches do enough in response to the genocide?" is more of an ethical question than a historical one. Nevertheless, accusations that the Canadian churches were too silent about the Jewish holocaust in the Second World War naturally raise the question of the churches' response to the Armenian genocide. In brief, the denominational press did make their readers aware of the disaster unfolding in Turkey, and, in a number of cases, supported fund-raising efforts for the Armenians. One might suggest that coverage of Armenian interests left something to be desired, but it must be remembered that Canadian readers were primarily focused on places where Canadians were affected, the Western Front and

---

80. "Transforming Mesopotamia," *Christian Guardian*, 7 November 1917, 4.

81. W. G. J., "The Reprisals of History," *Presbyterian and Westminster*, 5 December 1918, 509.

82. "The Fate of Turkey," *Presbyterian and Westminster*, 12 December 1918, 544. See also "Turkey Wants Peace," *Presbyterian Witness*, 21 September 1918, 4. Interestingly, one Methodist missionary publication called the Greeks "worse off" than they were under Turkish rule because their Christian leaders would not allow the Bible to be published in the vernacular. See "Missionary Notes," *The Missionary Outlook*, April 1916, 74; "Missionary Notes," *The Missionary Outlook*, July 1917, 146.

submarine attacks in the Atlantic. While one laments the dehumanizing constructions of the "Turk," what motivated such denunciations was the outrage against the Ottomans for the mistreatment of an ancient Christian people. As for the churches' support for the war effort, the war was portrayed as a war to end not just German militarism, but also Turkish misrule and massacres. Whatever one thinks today of the reasons for going to war in 1914–1918, surely waging a war that included the aim of ending a genocide in progress must have merit.

If the churches were guilty of anything, they were guilty of naivety, for believing that nations or empires act solely out of moral convictions. They appear to have believed that moral indignation was motivation enough for the Great Powers to fulfill their promises to the Armenians, but that was not—and rarely ever is—the case in politics. Lord Curzon's comment, "Oil weighed more heavily in the negotiations than Armenian blood,"[83] expresses his personal frustration with the abandonment of Armenia's interests in the postwar negotiations, and conveys the postwar realty of imperial agendas and political necessities trumping moral obligations.[84] It was not the churches that failed the Armenians. Western opinion had been appalled at the Armenian tragedy, and Western leaders such as Britain's Lloyd George had declared that the end of war would bring about the liberation and protection of the Armenians.[85] However, despite their professed good intentions, domestic and strategic considerations meant that no Western Power was willing to place troops on the ground and guarantee the protection of the Armenians. This failure, suggests G. S. Graber, implicates the French and British in the disaster in a way similar to the much-maligned Germans.[86]

The military success of Mustafa Kemal Ataturk in consolidating his control and defeating the Greeks in 1922 ultimately meant that the Entente Power's plans of Turkish partition were doomed and the Armenians abandoned to their fate. The Treaty of Lausanne (1923) mandated the compulsory exchange of minorities in Greece and Turkey, and this exchange is considered to be "the first organized transfer of large ethno-religious groups

83. As quoted in Somakian, *Empires in Conflict*, 176.

84. For a helpful summary of postwar political and imperial agendas, see Bloxham, *Game of Genocide*, ch. 4. For a contemporary example of politics trumping recognition of the genocide in Armenia, see Auron, *Banality of Denial*.

85. MacMillan, *Paris 1919*, 378.

86. Graber, *Caravans to Oblivion*, ch. 10.

"Thor and Allah . . . in a hideous, unholy confederacy"

by means of which minorities were forcibly uprooted under the aegis of international law to contribute, in turn, to the reconstruction of ethnically 'pure' homogenous states."[87] Not only did it deliver the final death blow to the church's presence in Asia Minor, it also meant the end of any hope for protection or restitution for the remaining Armenians.

Bibliography

Church Records

Assembly of the Presbyterian Church in Canada. "Fifteenth Sederunt." In *Acts and Proceedings of the Forty-Second General Assembly*, 47, 7–16 June 1916. In Presbyterian Archives, Toronto.

Newspapers

Canadian Baptist, 11 November 1915 to 26 December 1918. Canadian Baptist Archives, McMaster Divinity College.
Canadian Church Magazine and Mission News, 1896.
Canadian Churchman, October 1915 to December 1918. Anglican General Synod Archives, Toronto.
Christian Guardian, 1 September 1915 to 16 January 1918. Mills Library, McMaster University.
Diocesan Gazette, February-March 1917 to February 1918. Anglican Archives, Vancouver School of Theology.
Maritime Baptist, 6 October 1915 to 6 November 1918. Baptist Archives, Acadia University.
Mission World, January 1919. Anglican General Synod Archives, Toronto.
The Missionary Outlook, September 1915 to July 1918. United Church Archives, Toronto.
Montreal Churchman, September 1916 to January 1919. Anglican Archives, Montreal.
The Presbyterian, 26 October 1916. Presbyterian Archives, Toronto.
Presbyterian and Westminster, 27 December 1917 to 12 December 1918. Presbyterian Archives, Toronto.
Presbyterian Record, July 1917. Presbyterian Archives, Toronto.
Presbyterian Witness, 3 April 1915 to 21 September 1918. Presbyterian Archives, Toronto.
Queen's Quarterly, July-September 1917. Robarts Library, University of Toronto.
The Westminster, November 1915 to January 1916. Presbyterian Archives, Toronto.

Secondary Sources

Abella, Irving, and Harold Troper. *None Is Too Many: Canada and the Jews of Europe, 1933–1948*. Toronto: Lester & Orpen Dennys, 1982.

---

87. Yildirim, *Diplomacy and Displacement*, 10.

Akcam, Taner. *From Empire to Republic: Turkish Nationalism and the Armenian Genocide.* London: Zed, 2004.

Angus, Murray E. "Living in the 'World of the Tiger': The Methodist and Presbyterian Churches in Nova Scotia and the Great War, 1914–1918." MA thesis, Dalhousie University, 1993.

Arissian, Nora. "The Armenian Genocide in the Syrian Press." In *The Armenian Genocide: Cultural and Ethical Legacies,* edited by Richard G. Hovannisian, 303–7. New Brunswick, NJ: Transaction, 2008.

Armenian National Committee. *The Armenian Genocide as Reported in the Australian Press.* Sydney: Armenian National Committee, 1983.

Armenian National Institute. "Canadian House of Commons Resolution." No pages. 2012. Online: http://www.armenian-genocide.org/Affirmation.291/current_category.7/affirmation_detail.html

Armenian Youth Federation of Canada. *The Armenian Genocide in the Canadian Press.* Vol. 1, *1915–1916.* Montreal: Armenian National Committee of Canada, 1985.

Auron, Tair. *The Banality of Denial: Israel and the Armenian Genocide.* New Brunswick, NJ: Transaction, 2003.

Balakian, Peter. *The Burning Tigris: The Armenian Genocide and America's Response.* New York: HarperCollins, 2003.

Bardakjian, Kevork. *Hitler and the Armenian Genocide.* Cambridge, MA: Zoryan Institute, 1985.

Barton, James L., ed. *Turkish Atrocities: Statements of American Missionaries on the Destruction of Christian Communities in Ottoman Turkey, 1915–1917.* Armenian Genocide Documentation Series 2. Ann Arbor: Gomidas Institute, 1998.

Berger, Carl. *The Sense of Power: Studies in the Ideas of Canadian Imperialism, 1867–1914.* Toronto: University of Toronto Press, 1970.

Bloxham, Donald. *The Great Game of Genocide: Imperialism, Nationalism, and the Destruction of the Ottoman Armenians.* Oxford: Oxford University Press, 2005.

Bowler, Kate. "'We Wish to Inform You': Canadian Religious Reporting of the Rwandan Genocide." *Canadian Society of Church History Papers* (2008) 175–95.

Brewer, Charles G. "The Diocese of Antigonish and World War 1." MA thesis, University of New Brunswick, 1975.

Buckner, Philip. "Whatever Happened to the British Empire?" *Journal of the Canadian Historical Association* 4 (1993) 3–32.

———. "Canada." In *The Impact of the South African War,* edited by David Omissi and Andrew S. Thompson, 233–50. Houndmills, UK: Palgrave, 2002.

CBC News. "Turkey Condemns Canada's Armenian Genocide Vote." No pages. Online: http://www.cbc.ca/news/canada/story/2004/04/22/armenia040422.html

Cole, Douglas. "Canada's 'Nationalistic' Imperialists." *Journal of Canadian Studies* 5 (August 1970) 44–49.

Cook, Terry. "George R. Parkin and the Concept of Britannic Idealism." *Journal of Canadian Studies* 10 (August 1975) 15–31.

Dadrian, Vahakn N. *The History of the Armenian Genocide: Ethnic Conflict from the Balkans to Anatolia to the Caucasus.* New York: Berghahn, 1995.

Davidson, Melissa. "Preaching the Great War: Canadian Anglicans and the War Sermon, 1914–1918." MA thesis, McGill University, 2011.

Davis, Leslie A. *The Slaughterhouse Province: An American Diplomat's Report on the Armenian Genocide, 1915–1917.* New Rochelle, NY: Aristide D. Caratzas, 1989.

Dekmejian, R. Hrair. "Determinants of Genocide: Armenians and Jews as Case Studies." In *The Armenian Genocide in Perspective*, edited by Richard G. Hovannisian, 85–96. New Brunswick, NJ: Transaction, 1986.

Derderian, Katherine. "Common Fate, Different Experience: Gender-Specific Aspects of the Armenian Genocide, 1915–1917." *Holocaust and Genocide Studies* 19 (2005) 1–25.

Dobkin, Marjorie Housepian. "What Genocide? What Holocaust? News from Turkey, 1915–1923: A Case Study." In *The Armenian Genocide in Perspective*, edited by Richard G. Hovannisian, 97–109. New Brunswick, NJ: Transaction, 1986.

Ferguson, Niall. *The War of the World: History's Age of Hatred*. London: Penguin, 2006.

Fowler, Michelle. "Keeping the Faith: The Presbyterian Press in Peace and War, 1913–1919." MA thesis, Wilfrid Laurier University, 2005.

Genizi, Haim. *The Holocaust, Israel, and the Canadian Protestant Churches*. Montreal and Kingston: McGill-Queen's University Press, 2002.

Graber, G. S. *Caravans to Oblivion: The Armenian Genocide, 1915*. New York: John Wiley, 1996.

Guant, David. *Massacres, Resistance, Protectors: Muslim-Christian Relations in Eastern Anatolia during World War I*. Piscataway, NJ: Gorgias, 2006.

Guroian, Vigen. "Collective Responsibility and Official Excuse Making: The Case of the Turkish Genocide of the Armenians." In *The Armenian Genocide in Perspective*, edited by Richard G. Hovannisian, 135–52. New Brunswick, NJ: Transaction, 1986.

Heath, Gordon L., ed. *Canadian Churches and the First World War*. Eugene, OR: Pickwick, 2014.

———. "Canadian Churches and War: An Introductory Essay and Annotated Bibliography." *McMaster Journal of Theology and Ministry* 12 (2010–2011) 61–124.

———. "'Citizens of That Mighty Empire': Imperial Sentiment among Students at Wesley College, 1897–1902." *Manitoba History* 49 (June 2005) 15–25.

———. "'Forming Sound Public Opinion': The Late Victorian Canadian Protestant Press and Nation-Building." *Journal of the Canadian Church Historical Society* 48 (2006) 109–59.

———. "Passion for Empire: War Poetry Published in the Canadian English Protestant Press during the South African War, 1899–1902." *Literature and Theology* 16 (2002) 127–47.

———. "Sin in the Camp: The Day of Humble Supplication in the Anglican Church in Canada in the Early Months of the South African War." *Journal of the Canadian Church Historical Society* 44 (2002) 207–26.

———. *A War with a Silver Lining: Canadian Protestant Churches and the South African War, 1899–1902*. Montreal and Kingston: McGill-Queen's University Press, 2009.

———. "'Were We in the Habit of Deifying Monarchs': Canadian English Protestants and the Death of Queen Victoria, 1901." *Canadian Evangelical Review* (Fall 2005–Spring 2006) 72–97.

Hofmann, Tessa. "German Eyewitness Reports of the Genocide of the Armenians, 1915–16." In *A Crime of Silence: The Armenian Genocide, the Permanent People's Tribunal*, edited by Gerard Libaridian, 61–92. London: Zed, 1985.

Hopkins, J. Castell. *The Sword of Islam, or Suffering Armenia: Annals of Turkish Power and the Eastern Question*. Brantford: Bradley-Garretson, 1896.

Hovannisian, Richard G. "The Armenian Genocide and Patterns of Denial." In *The Armenian Genocide in Perspective*, edited by Richard G. Hovannisian, 111–33. New Brunswick, NJ: Transaction, 1986.

———, ed. *The Armenian Genocide in Perspective*. New Brunswick, NJ: Transaction, 1986.

———, ed. *The Armenian Genocide: Cultural and Ethical Legacies*. New Brunswick, NJ: Transaction, 2008.

———. "Bitter-Sweet Memories: The Last Generation of Ottoman Armenians." In *Looking Backward, Moving Forward: Confronting the Armenian Genocide*, edited by Richard G. Hovannisian, 113–24. New Brunswick, NJ: Transaction, 2003.

———. "Denial of the Armenian Genocide in Comparison with Holocaust Denial." In *Remembrance and Denial: The Case of the Armenian Genocide*, edited by Richard G. Hovannisian. Detroit: Wayne State University Press, 1998.

———. "The Historical Dimensions of the Armenian Question, 1878–1923." In *The Armenian Genocide in Perspective*, edited by Richard G. Hovannisian, 19–41. New Brunswick, NJ: Transaction, 1986.

———, ed. *Looking Backward, Moving Forward: Confronting the Armenian Genocide*. New Brunswick, NJ: Transaction, 2003.

———, ed. *Remembrance and Denial: The Case of the Armenian Genocide*. Detroit: Wayne State University Press, 1998.

Jenkins, Philip. *The Lost History of Christianity: The Thousand-Year Golden Age of the Church in the Middle East, Africa, and Asia—and How It Died*. New York: HarperCollins, 2008.

Kaiser, Hilmar. "The Baghdad Railway and the Armenian Genocide, 1915–1916." In *Remembrance and Denial: The Case of the Armenian Genocide*, edited by Richard G. Hovannisian, 67–112. Detroit: Wayne State University Press, 1998.

Khosroeva, Anahit. "The Assyrian Genocide in the Ottoman Empire and Adjacent Territories." In *The Armenian Genocide: Cultural and Ethical Legacies*, edited by Richard G. Hovannisian, 267–74. New Brunswick, NJ: Transaction, 2008.

Kiernan, Ben. "Twentieth Century Genocides: Underlying Ideological Themes from Armenia to East Timor." In *The Specter of Genocide: Mass Murder in Historical Perspective*, edited by Robert Gellately and Ben Kiernan. Cambridge: Cambridge University Press, 2003.

Kirakossian, Arman J. *The Armenian Massacres 1894–1896: British Media Testimony*. Dearborn: Armenian Research Center, 2008.

———. *The Armenian Massacres 1894–1896: U.S. Media Testimony*. Detroit: Wayne State University Press, 2004.

———. *British Diplomacy and the Armenian Question, from the 1830s to 1914*. Princeton: Gomidas Institute, 2003.

Kloian, Richard, ed. *The Armenian Genocide: News Accounts from the American Press*. Berkeley: Anto, 1985.

Kuper, Leo. "The Turkish Genocide of Armenians, 1915–1917." In *The Armenian Genocide in Perspective*, edited by Richard G. Hovannisian, 43–59. New Brunswick, NJ: Transaction, 1986.

Lewy, Guenter. *The Armenian Massacres in Ottoman Turkey: A Disputed Genocide*. Salt Lake City: University of Utah Press, 2005.

MacDonald, Stuart. "From Just War to Crusade: The Wartime Sermons of the Rev. Thomas Eakin." MDiv thesis, Knox College, 1985.

MacMillan, Margaret. *Paris 1919*. New York: Random House, 2003.

Marashlian, Levon. "Finishing the Genocide: Cleansing Turkey of Armenian Survivors, 1920–1923." In *Remembrance and Denial: The Case of the Armenian Genocide*, edited by Richard G. Hovannisian, 113–45. Detroit: Wayne State University Press, 1998.

Melson, Robert. "Provocation or Nationalism: A Critical Inquiry into the Armenian Genocide of 1915." In *The Armenian Genocide in Perspective*, edited by Richard G. Hovannisian, 61–84. New Brunswick, NJ: Transaction, 1986.

Millennium Assembly of the United Nations. "Convention on the Prevention and Punishment of the Crime of Genocide." No pages. 2011. Online: http://www.un.org/millennium/law/iv-1.htm

Miller, Carman. "English-Canadian Opposition to the South African War as Seen through the Press." *Canadian Historical Review* 55 (1974) 422–38.

Miller, Donald E., and Lorna Touryan. "Armenian Survivors: A Typological Analysis of Victim Response." *Oral History Review* 10 (1982) 47–72.

———. "An Oral History Perspective on Responses to the Armenian Genocide." In *The Armenian Genocide in Perspective*, edited by Richard G. Hovannisian, 187–203. New Brunswick, NJ: Transaction, 1986.

———. *Survivors: An Oral History of the Armenian Genocide*. Berkeley: University of California Press, 1993.

Moranian, Suzanne E. "A Legacy of Paradox: U.S. Foreign Policy and the Armenian Genocide." In *The Armenian Genocide: Cultural and Ethical Legacies*, edited by Richard G. Hovannisian, 309–24. New Brunswick, NJ: Transaction, 2008.

Nassibian, Akaby. *Britain and the Armenian Question, 1915–1923*. London: Croom Helm, 1984.

Nefsky, Alan Davies, and Marilyn Felcher. "The Church of England in Canada and the Jewish Plight during the Nazi Era, 1933–1945." *Canadian Jewish Historical Society Journal* 10 (1988) 1–19.

———. *How Silent Were the Churches? Canadian Protestantism and the Jewish Plight during the Nazi Era*. Waterloo: Wilfrid Laurier University Press, 1997.

———. "The United Church and the Jewish Plight during the Nazi Era, 1933–1945." *Canadian Jewish Historical Society Journal* 8 (1984) 55–72.

Nichanian, Marc. "The Truth of the Facts." In *Remembrance and Denial: The Case of the Armenian Genocide*, edited by Richard G. Hovannisian, 249–70. Detroit: Wayne State University Press, 1998.

Oke, Mim Kemal. *The Armenian Question, 1914–1923*. Nicosia, Cyprus: K. Rustem, 1988.

Olusoga, David, and Casper W. Erichsen. *The Kaiser's Holocaust: Germany's Forgotten Genocide and the Colonial Roots of Nazism*. London: Faber & Faber, 2010.

Ostergaard, Karen. "Canadian Nationalism and Anti-Imperialism, 1896–1911." PhD diss., Dalhousie University, 1976.

Page, Robert. *The Boer War and Canadian Imperialism*. Ottawa: The Canadian Historical Association, 1987.

———. "Canada and the Imperial Idea in the Boer War Years." *Journal of Canadian Studies* 5 (February 1970) 33–49.

———. "Carl Berger and the Intellectual Origins of Canadian Imperialist Thought, 1867–1914." *Journal of Canadian Studies* 5 (August 1970) 39–43.

Payaslian, Simon. "The United States Response to the Armenian Genocide." In *Looking Backward, Moving Forward: Confronting the Armenian Genocide*, edited by Richard G. Hovannisian, 51–80. New Brunswick, NJ: Transaction, 2003.

Penlington, Norman. *Canada and Imperialism, 1896.* Toronto: University of Toronto Press, 1965.

Peroomian, Rubina. "Problematic Aspects of Reading Genocide Literature: A Search for a Guideline or a Canon." In *Remembrance and Denial: The Case of the Armenian Genocide,* edited by Richard G. Hovannisian, 175–86. Detroit: Wayne State University Press, 1998.

Peterson, Merrill D. *"Starving Armenians," America and the Armenian Genocide, 1915–1930 and After.* Charlottesville: University of Virginia Press, 2004.

Richards, Samuel J. "Ministry of Propaganda: Canadian Methodists, Empire, and Loyalty in World War I." MA thesis, Salisbury University, 2007.

Sarafian, Ara. "The Archival Trail: Authentication of the Treatment of Armenians in the Ottoman Empire, 1915–16." In *Remembrance and Denial: The Case of the Armenian Genocide,* edited by Richard G. Hovannisian, 51–65. Detroit: Wayne State University Press, 1998.

Semple, Neil. *The Lord's Dominion: The History of Canadian Methodism.* Montreal and Kingston: McGill-Queen's University Press, 1996.

Shantz, Mary-Ann. "Kingston Christians and the Persecution of European Jews during the Nazi Era." *Canadian Society of Church History Papers* (1992) 5–18.

Shirinian, Lorne. *Quest for Closure: The Armenian Genocide and the Search for Justice in Canada.* Kingston: Blue Heron, 1999.

———. "Survivor Memoirs of the Armenian Genocide as Cultural History." In *Remembrance and Denial: The Case of the Armenian Genocide,* edited by Richard G. Hovannisian, 165–73. Detroit: Wayne State University Press, 1998.

Silver, A. I. "Some Quebec Attitudes in an Age of Imperialism and Ideological Conflict." *Canadian Historical Review* 57 (1976) 441–60.

Smith, Roger W., Eric Markusen, and Robert Jay Lifton. "Professional Ethics and the Denial of the Armenian Genocide." In *Remembrance and Denial: The Case of the Armenian Genocide,* edited by Richard G. Hovannisian, 271–95. Detroit: Wayne State University Press, 1998.

Somakian, Manoug Joseph. *Empires in Conflict: Armenia and the Great Powers, 1895–1920.* London: Tauris, 1995.

Ternon, Yves. "Freedom and Responsibility of the Historian: The 'Lewis Affair.'" In *Remembrance and Denial: The Case of the Armenian Genocide,* 237–48. Detroit: Wayne State University Press, 1998.

Theriault, Henry C. "Denial and Free Speech: The Case of the Armenian Genocide." In *Looking Backward, Moving Forward: Confronting the Armenian Genocide,* edited by Richard G. Hovannisian, 231–61. New Brunswick, NJ: Transaction, 2003.

Videlier, Philippe. "French Society and the Armenian Genocide." In *The Armenian Genocide: Cultural and Ethical Legacies,* edited by Richard G. Hovannisian, 325–33. New Brunswick, NJ: Transaction, 2008.

Walker, C. J. *Armenia: The Survival of a Nation.* London: Croom Helm, 1980.

Weitz, Eric D. *A Century of Genocide: Utopias of Race and Nation.* Princeton: Princeton University Press, 2003.

Winter, Jay, ed. *America and the Armenian Genocide of 1915.* Cambridge: Cambridge University Press, 2003.

Yildirim, Onur. *Diplomacy and Displacement: Reconsidering the Turco-Greek Exchange of Populations, 1922–1934.* New York: Routledge, 2006.

8

A Theology of Persecution and Martyrdom
An Example in Globalizing Theology

CHRISTOF SAUER

MUCH OF POPULAR MISSIOLOGY in recent decades has been dominated by lopsided emphases: sometimes by a managerial missiology,[1] asking "what must we organize?" and at other times by a pragmatic missiology, claiming "if it works, it must be good." These approaches have in common a tendency towards a "theology of glory and success," often at the expense of a "theology of the cross." The reality of suffering, persecution, or martyrdom is often bypassed. However, according to the latest sociological research, two-thirds of the world's population lives in countries with serious restrictions on religious freedom. Christians in these countries number at least 200 million.[2] The focus of this chapter is theological reflection on such persecution and martyrdom, not the reality itself.

Rarely have Western theologies engaged with the reality of suffering, persecution, and martyrdom for Christ and their significance for mission.

---

1. For a criticism of the reduction of world missions to a managerial enterprise, cf. Engel and Dyrness, *Changing the Mind*, 67–74.

2. For the most comprehensive descriptions of persecution of Christians, see Boyd-MacMillan, *Faith that Endures*, and for restrictions on religious freedom, see Marshall, *Religious Freedom*, and the publications of the Pew Forum on Religion and Public Life: *Global Restrictions*, and *Rising Restrictions*. On the various approaches for researching persecution, see Sauer, "Researching Persecution." See also the websites of the International Institute for Religious Freedom (IIRF) and the US Department of State, as well as advocacy agencies.

From a Western perspective, persecution is often something associated with the past. A few might know it is happening elsewhere, but the general assumption seems to be, "it will never happen here."[3] So the topic seems irrelevant and is largely ignored by Western theology. But who says that the Western perspective is all-sufficient, normative, or the decisive one? Ought not a contemporary theology seriously explore a topic that is of very obvious, immediate, and painful relevance to large parts of global Christianity? After all, it is also a topic that permeates Scripture. Could it be that on closer study the topic might be of more relevance for us than we think, and that an exercise in globalizing theology might uncover some of our blind spots and correct our own theology?

In September 2009, an international group of theologians and missiologists gathered in the German town Bad Urach to develop an evangelical theology of suffering, persecution, and martyrdom for the global church in mission.[4] A major rationale for this consultation was that the church seemed ill-equipped for the suffering that comes with its mission in the world.[5] The participants issued their findings in the eighty-page *Bad Urach Statement* with the subtitle "Towards an Evangelical Theology of Suffering, Persecution, and Martyrdom for the Global Church in Mission."[6] This chapter is an introduction to some of its conclusions, and an invitation for readers to examine them in an exercise in global theology.

This chapter only sketches the theological core of the consultation statement, giving an outline of a theology of persecution and martyrdom. The entire statement is much more detailed and deals with a number of other perspectives. It tries to overcome current misperceptions and distorted terminology concerning suffering, persecution, and martyrdom. It also responds to them extensively from the ethical perspectives of the individual, the local church, parachurch organizations, and the global

---

3. For a detailed discussion on current (mis-)perceptions on persecution, see Tieszen, *Re-examining Religious Persecution*, 17–36.

4. The consultation was organized by the IIRF (www.iirf.eu), sponsored by the World Evangelical Alliance Religious Liberty Commission, in co-operation with a number of other commissions.

5. Cf. World Evangelical Alliance's "Statement on Prosperity Theology."

6. The *Bad Urach Statement* has been summarized in "The Bad Urach Call," which is a short and more popular appeal. Both can be found at www.iirf.eu and are published as part of the compendium on the Bad Urach Consultation: Sauer and Howell, eds., *Suffering, Persecution and Martyrdom*.

A Theology of Persecution and Martyrdom

Christian community. Finally it recommends practical applications both for Christian mission and for theological education.

The Drama of God's History with the World (Hermeneutical Dimensions)

Obviously, the way we view Scripture influences what we find in it. Only a comprehensive view of God's cosmic plans, as far as they are revealed in Scripture, will help us to interpret suffering, persecution, and martyrdom and their relation to mission properly. A salvation-historical approach to interpreting the Bible and to doing theology seems very helpful in this regard.[7] The suffering of the church for Christ is so much a part of its mission in the period between Christ's ascension and his *parousia* that suffering has been declared a mark of the church by theologians.[8]

Old Testament Models of Faithfulness (Typological Dimensions)

In contemporary Christianity, it is quite common to bypass the Old Testament and go straight to the New Testament on any issue. This practice is an unfortunate oversight because the Old Testament shows that suffering, persecution, and martyrdom have been the lot of God's people over and over again, beginning with the martyrdom of Abel. Job exemplifies the suffering of the righteous allowed by God, and he serves as a typology of Christ. Conflict, persecution, and martyrdom were all characteristics of the true prophets (Neh 9:26; Matt 23:37). Israel, as the elect people of God, on the one hand had to suffer for their calling at the hands of the nations, beginning with slavery in Egypt. On the other hand, it should be noted that often the cause of Israel's suffering was God's punishment for Israel's unfaithfulness to Yahweh (e.g., Lev 26:14–39).

---

7. In exegesis, Oscar Cullmann propagated this approach. Peter Beyerhaus did so in missiology.

8. See, for example, Luther, "On the Councils," 164.

Christ, the Suffering Servant (Christological Dimensions)

Jesus Christ as the center of Christian faith plays the normative role in the Christian view of suffering, persecution, and martyrdom. Therefore, the interpretation of Jesus' life and death is crucial. The way of Jesus the Messiah, through suffering to glory, is exemplary for his disciples. All Christian martyrdom has its basic foundational orientation and footing in Jesus Christ, the "faithful and true witness" (Rev 1:5; 3:14; cf. 1 Pet 2:21–24; Heb 2:14–18; 5:8). From his infancy, Jesus was persecuted (Matt 2:13–14), and his first sermon met with bitter resistance (Luke 4:14–30). Finally, he stood up as a witness to the truth during his questioning before the judges (John 18:37). To Jesus, the crucifixion was not at all the tragic failure of his mission, but rather its very fulfillment.

Discipleship: Following in the Footsteps of Christ (Mimetic Dimensions)

A key question in any theology of martyrdom is how the cross of Christ relates to the cross of his disciples. The death of Jesus on the cross is unique and at the same time serves as a model for his followers. It was unique in that it was an atoning sacrifice for the sins of the world, completely sufficient, irreplaceable, unrepeatable. It cannot be duplicated. However, the unique nature of Jesus' suffering does not negate the fact that Jesus gave his followers a model to follow.[9] Christian suffering for Christ is a continuation of the suffering of Christ, and it is from him only that it receives its characteristic mark (John 17:18; 20:21). His disciples are treated today as he once was, because Christ lives in them and they speak and act with his authority. Their fate is united with his. The core meaning of taking up one's cross to be a disciple of Jesus (Luke 9:23) is witnessing for Jesus Christ, even in a situation of persecution and martyrdom.[10]

---

9. Lee, "God's Mission in Suffering."
10. Penner, *In the Shadow*, 116–54.

A Theology of Persecution and Martyrdom

SUPER-HUMAN CONFLICT (ANTAGONISTIC DIMENSIONS)

There is a dimension to persecution and martyrdom that cannot be appropriately assessed by means of the social sciences. From a theological perspective, the world's hatred toward Christians is ultimately inspired by Satan's even deeper hatred of them; he has been fighting against God ever since his primeval rebellion. Because Jesus totally stripped him of his power on Calvary, the anger of the dark powers is directed completely against Jesus and all who confess him.

Jesus saw his ministry as an assault on the rule of Satan in the world with the purpose of bringing in the rule of God through the kingdom of God. Jesus was sent as the Lamb of God to defeat the great dragon and to destroy his works (1 John 3:8). In the same way, he sends his followers as lambs to defeat the wolves by transforming them into children of God. Christ's ultimate weapon is self-sacrifice and our ultimate weapon must be the same, in order to draw people to Jesus (John 12:24, 26, 32).[11]

The church suffers because the world, in rebellion against God, hates Christ (cf. John 15:20a). It is difficult to explain fully the irrational brutality of the persecution of Christians without recourse to the demonic. In the midst of the stark reality of this conflict, the church can be assured that no enemy or adversity is able to separate the believer from the love of Christ (Rom 8:31–39).[12]

GOD'S SALVATION AND COMFORT (SOTERIOLOGICAL DIMENSIONS)

Jesus points out the seriousness of remaining faithful to him and confessing him in moments of trial. Those who endure to the end and remain victorious will be saved (Matt 24:13; Rev 21:7–8). While the Father, the Son, and the Holy Spirit, as well as God's angels, comfort and help the afflicted Christian (2 Cor 1:3–11; Heb 2:18; Matt 10:17; Acts 5:18), God's helping presence does not dispense with personal responsibility to bear and to stand fast. Neither does his helping presence necessarily spare the lives of those being afflicted. Some Christians, like James (Acts 12:2), receive God's help to remain faithful, despite torture and execution.

---

11. Ton, "Suffering and Martyrdom," 201–204.
12. Sauer, *Mission und Martyrium*, 101.

There remains the question of what the suffering and martyrdom of a Christian can contribute to the salvation of others (Col 1:24; 2 Tim 2:10; Phil 1:12–26). Although the work of the messianic martyr Jesus is complete, Christ's suffering in the members of his body is not yet so (Rev 6:11). Paul's apostolic suffering is "instrumental" suffering,[13] because it serves to bring the gospel to those who need to be saved, and to keep faithful those who have been saved.

The Body of Christ (Ecclesiological Dimensions)

Thus far in the history of the Christian faith, some Christians have always been more intensely persecuted than others. This circumstance begs the question, how should those facing intense persecution and those facing mild persecution relate to one another? Christians never suffer alone and Christian martyrs never die alone because they are always a part of the body of Christ that sustains them. The body of Christ needs to be understood in three dimensions: across time, across space, and across denominations. The Christian confessors and martyrs, of the past and the present, need to be rightly remembered. Those who are currently suffering are to remember that Christians all over the world are going through the same kind of suffering (1 Pet 5:9). The body of Christ that is present in the world at a given time participates in the suffering of its various members by sharing their stories, praying, supporting, suffering, and rejoicing with them. If one part of the body suffers, all parts are equally concerned (1 Cor 12:26). When Christians of different confessions and denominations suffer together for Christ, it creates the potential for building ecumenical solidarity. A complication is added in cases where one Christian group is, or has been, persecuting another Christian group or has been complicit with government repression against other groups. In such cases a healing of memories is necessary.

A further point in these ecclesiological dimensions concerns group egoisms. Advocacy for persecuted Christians must never be sectarian, only focusing on those from one's own denomination or confession and ignoring the plight of those with differing theological convictions. Martyrdom serves to build up the church because those suffering and martyred are blessed by God.[14]

---

13. The term was coined by Lee, "God's Mission in Suffering," 46–55.
14. ICN, "Readiness to Suffer"; Beyerhaus, "Martyrdom."

God's Mission for the Church (Missiological Dimensions)

Suffering and martyrdom are not ends in themselves, but serve God's mission right to the end of time (Matt 24:9–14). The suffering and the weakness of the witness are a mode of mission (2 Cor 4:7–10; 12:9–10), and martyrdom becomes the most radical form of witness. Witness to Christ is a core cause of suffering. While we might be perfect in contextualizing our message and in avoiding any unnecessary offense, as messengers of Christ we must face the fact that the message of the cross has been, and always will be, a stumbling block to those without Christ (1 Cor 1:18, 23), and will attract the hostility of the world that does not accept the light coming into the world (John 1:4, 11). Our willingness to suffer for our mission makes its genuineness plausible. Suffering is not just a mishap to be avoided at all cost.

Tertullian's widely quoted saying, *"semen est sanguis Christianorum"*[15] (the blood of the martyrs is the seed of the church), is often taken out of context and given a triumphalistic undertone, but it nonetheless gives rise to the important question of how persecution and church growth are related. Does persecution automatically and always lead to church growth? Or is it rather that the growth of the church leads to persecution? Or is it even more complex than that?

A theologically responsible position must recognize the complexity and vagaries of history as well as the mystery of God's providence: even the catastrophes of world history seem to be used by God as vehicles for the progress of his kingdom. Those who suffer for Christ can give a convincing message. While the seed that falls into the ground will bear much fruit over time according to God's promise, martyrdom does not automatically produce visible and immediate church growth. The "fruit" of martyrdom remains a grace from God (John 12:24). In some places persecution has led to the expansion of the church, but in others heavy persecution has completely destroyed or marginalized it.[16] Martyrdom brings to a violent end the voice of a particular witness and might discourage the witness of others, or silence the last and only witness in a given area.

---

15. Tertullian, *Apology* 50.13.
16. For instance, see Heath, "When the Blood of the Martyrs Was Not Enough."

The Victory of the Kingdom of God (Eschatological Dimensions)

What then should Christian expectations be regarding the future? The period in which we live is marked by the tension between the victory of Christ that has already been accomplished and its visible consummation that has not yet taken place (Matt 5:45; Rom 8:19–22). Because Christ was raised from death, ascended to heaven, and was installed as sovereign, Christians may rightly hope for a resurrection to a better life. The promise of resurrection provides a reason to stand firm and immovable in affliction, and affirmation that work for God is not in vain, though deadly forces might seemingly destroy it (1 Cor 15:58).

In contrast to optimistic visions of the future involving seamless transformation, the prophecies of the Bible foresee clearly an altogether troubled final stage of human and church history (Deut 7; 1 Thess 2; 2 Tim 3:1–13; Rev 13–19). Both the worldwide proclamation of the gospel to all ethnic groups and worldwide distress will reach a climax (Matt 24:9–25; Rev 6:9–11; 17:6) with the passing away of the old world and the completion of the new. These prophecies encourage each generation to discern and endure historically and locally-restricted forms of persecution in their own times as anticipations on a smaller scale of what is to come (1 John 2:18).[17]

Christians should not focus on the horrors of the coming end times, but instead should joyfully[18] expect their returning Lord, as bridegroom, judge, and king (Rev 19:6–10; 21:1–5; 16:5–6). God is not in a hurry with his final victory. Rather he is patient with humankind because he does not want anyone to perish, but wants to give everyone an opportunity for repentance (2 Pet 3:4, 9).

The Honor of God and His Martyrs (Doxological Dimensions)

In the end, the crucial question is, what does God think of martyrdom? God is honored both by the life and by the death of his witnesses (Rom 14:8; 12:1; Phil 1:20; Acts 20:24). God is honored by the witness in weakness (2 Cor 12:9–10) to a seemingly foolish gospel (1 Cor 1:18, 31), and the faithfulness of the martyrs (John 21:18–19), as well as by the church's

---

17. ICN, "Readiness to Suffer."
18. Fernando, *Call to Joy and Pain*.

A Theology of Persecution and Martyrdom

confidence in his reign (Acts 4:2–30), and the conversion of persecutors (1 Pet 2:12; Phil 2:6–11). Honoring God is the eternal destiny of God's children (Rev 7:9–17; 15:2–4; 19:2). The glorification of God is the ultimate goal of mission, and everything must in the end serve his glory.

This leads to some pressing questions: Does God reward faithfulness? When and how? God bestows his glory already in this life on those who suffer for him, allows some martyrs a glimpse of his glory in their hour of trial, and in heaven lets them share the glory of Christ (1 Pet 4:14; Acts 7:55). In other words, those who are martyred are led through temporal suffering to eternal glory and are honored by God (1 Pet 1:11; Heb 2:9; Rom 8:17–18; 1 Pet 4:13–14).

The Bible also promises a heavenly reward to the faithful.[19] The character formation and the testing of a Christian's faithfulness accomplished in suffering, persecution, or martyrdom for Christ have clear corresponding results in heaven (Rev 3:12, 21; 20:4; Luke 22:28–30; 2 Cor 4:17). The content of the promised reward is being heirs with Christ, being glorified with him (Rom 8:17), and reigning with him (2 Tim 2:12). These promises are a great source of inspiration, courage, and strength for the Christians who are called to face persecution and martyrdom. Suffering and martyrdom are not human achievements to boast about; it is the grace of God that enables one to go victoriously through such sufferings.

Conclusion

The authors of the *Bad Urach Statement* are specifically calling on theologians, missiologists, and Christian leaders to consider their message in view of fulfilling together in joint obedience the mission to which God has called all Christians. They encourage fellow Christians to study the *Bad Urach Statement* personally in the light of Scripture, to assess what relevance it has for ministry, and to reflect how this statement could be used at one's level of responsibility. In regards to a globalizing theology and the *Bad Urach Statement*, I see a need to move forward in two directions. First, more non-Western theologians need to be discovered who have reflected on the issues raised by the statement.[20] Such theologians would have the potential

---

19. Ton, *Suffering, Martyrdom and Rewards*.

20. The contributing works of those who have participated in the discussion process surrounding the Bad Urach Consultation, in addition to those cited already in this essay, include Adiwardana, "Training Missionaries"; Bosch, *Spirituality of the Road*

to address deficits in Western theology in a more differentiated manner, for unearthing treasures hidden in obscurity or behind language barriers is a worthwhile endeavor.[21] Second, this exercise in globalizing theology has thus far remained within the evangelical tradition. At the consultation in Bad Urach we discussed the need to engage in conversations with tradition such as the Oriental and Eastern Orthodox or Roman Catholic, as well as movements such as liberation theology. In conclusion, I personally want to encourage all readers to pursue witnessing boldly for the crucified and risen Christ, even in the face of suffering, persecution, and martyrdom, and doing so humbly, inspired, and enabled by Christ to loving sacrifice.

Bibliography

Adiwardana, Margaretha. "Training Missionaries to Persevere: Holistic Preparation for Situations of Adversity." MTh diss., DTC Singapore, 1999.

Beyerhaus, Peter P. J. "Martyrdom—Gate to the Kingdom of Heaven." In *God's Kingdom and the Utopian Error: Discerning the Biblical Kingdom of God from Its Political Counterfeits*, 163–79. Wheaton: Crossway, 1992.

Bosch, David J. *A Spirituality of the Road*. 1979. Reprint, Eugene, OR: Wipf & Stock, 2000.

———. *Transforming Mission*. Maryknoll: Orbis, 1991.

Boyd-MacMillan, Ronald. *Faith that Endures: The Essential Guide to the Persecuted Church*. Lancaster: Sovereign World, 2006. [Available via Open Doors Canada].

Dau, Isaiah Majok. *Suffering and God. A Theological Reflection on the War in Sudan*. Nairobi: Paulines, 2002.

Engel, James F., and William A. Dyrness. *Changing the Mind of World Missions: Where Have We Gone Wrong?* Downers Grove, IL: InterVarsity, 2000.

Fernando, Ajith. *The Call to Joy and Pain: Embracing Suffering in Your Ministry*. Wheaton: Crossway, 2007.

Global Restrictions on Religion. Washington DC: Pew Forum on Religion and Public Life, 2009. Online: http://pewforum.org/docs/DocID=491

Grim, Brian J. "Religious Freedom." In *Atlas of Global Christianity 1910–2010*, edited by Todd M. Johnson et al., 36–42. Edinburgh: Edinburgh University Press, 2009.

Heath, Gordon L. "When the Blood of the Martyrs Was Not Enough: A Survey of Places Where the Church Was Wiped Out." In *The Church, Then and Now*, edited by Stanley E. Porter and Cynthia Westfall, 97–133. Eugene, OR: Pickwick, 2012.

---

and *Transforming Mission*; Dau, *Suffering and God*; Grim, "Religious Freedom"; Schirrmacher, *Persecution of Christians*; Sookhdeo, *Persecuted Church*; Sterk, "Dynamics of Persecution"; Taylor, van der Meer, and Reimer, *Mission in Contexts of Suffering*; van der Meer, "Understanding and Supporting Missionaries"; Wespetal, "Marytrdom". See also the 1974 Lausanne Covenant (online: www.lausanne.org).

21. One such hidden treasure largely unknown outside the German-speaking world is the missiological interpretation of suffering for Christ by Karl Hartenstein. See Sauer, "Towards a Theology of 'Mission under the Cross.'"

ICN. "Readiness to Suffer for Christ." 1996. Online: www.institut-diakrisis.de/PDEnglishVersion.pdf.
Lee, Young Kee. "God's Mission in Suffering and Martyrdom." PhD diss., Fuller Theological Seminary, School of World Mission, 1999.
Luther, Martin. "On the Councils and the Church." In *Luther's Works*, edited by Eric W. Gitsch, translated by Charles M. Jacobs, 13–178. Philadelphia: Fortress, 1966.
Marshall, Paul A., ed. *Religious Freedom in the World*. Lanham: Rowman & Littlefield, 2008.
Penner, Glenn. *In the Shadow of the Cross: A Biblical Theology of Persecution and Discipleship*. Bartlesville, OK: Living Sacrifice, 2004.
Rising Restrictions on Religion. Washington DC: Pew Forum on Religion and Public Life, 2011. Online: http://pewforum.org/Government/Rising-Restrictions-on-Religion.aspx.
Sauer, Christof. *Mission und Martyrium*. Bonn: VKW, 1994.
―――. "Researching Persecution and Martyrdom." *International Journal for Religious Freedom* 1 (2008) 26–48.
―――. "Towards a Theology of 'Mission under the Cross': A Contribution from Germany by Karl Hartenstein." In *Suffering, Persecution and Martyrdom*, edited by Christof Sauer et al., 257–85. Kempton Park, South Africa: AcadSA/Bonn: VKW, 2010.
Sauer, Christof, and Richard Howell, eds. *Suffering, Persecution and Martyrdom. Theological Reflections*. Kempton Park, South Africa: AcadSA/Bonn: VKW, 2010.
Schirrmacher, Thomas. *The Persecution of Christians Concerns Us All. Towards a Theology of Martyrdom*. 2001. Reprint, Bonn: VKW, 2008. Online: www.iirf.eu.
Sookhdeo, Patrick, ed. *The Persecuted Church*. (Lausanne Occasional Paper No. 32). Kempton Park, South Africa: AcadSA, 2005 (African edition 2007). Online: www.lausanne.org.
"Statement on Prosperity Theology and Theology of Suffering by the Theological Commission of the World Evangelical Alliance (WEA) in 1994." *Evangelical Review of Theology* 20, no. 1 (1996) 5–13.
Sterk, Vernon Jay. "The Dynamics of Persecution." PhD diss., Fuller Theological Seminary, 1992.
Taylor, Willam D., Tonica van der Meer, and Reg Reimer, eds. *Mission in Contexts of Suffering, Violence, Persecution and Martyrdom*. Pasadena: William Carey Library, 2012.
Tieszen, Charles. *Re-examining Religious Persecution: Constructing a Theological Framework for Understanding Persecution*. Kempton Park, South Africa: AcadSA, 2008. Online: www.iirf.eu.
Ton, Josef. *Suffering, Martyrdom and Rewards in Heaven*. Lanham, MD: University Press of America, 1997. 2nd ed., Oradea, Romania: Cartea Crestina, 2007. [Available via Romanian Missionary Society, 1825 College Ave. #188, P.O. Box 527, Wheaton, IL USA, 60189; Webstore: http://rms.revtrak.net/tek9.asp]
―――. "Suffering and Martyrdom: A Defining and Essential Christian Characteristic." In *Suffering, Persecution and Martyrdom*, edited by Christof Sauer et al., 199–214. Kempton Park, South Africa: AcadSA/Bonn: VKW, 2010.
van der Meer, Antonia Leonora. "Understanding and Supporting Missionaries Serving in Contexts of Suffering." DMiss diss., Asia Graduate School of Theology, Philippines, 2005.
Wespetal, Thomas J. "Martyrdom and the Furtherance of God's Plan: The Value of Dying for the Christian Faith." PhD diss., Trinity Evangelical Divinity School, 2005.

9

Global Christianity
Eyewitness Reflections from Iraq, Kenya, and South Korea

John Haitham Issak,

David Kirwa Tarus,

Seongho Kang

Iraq: Fr. John Haitham Issak

Many significant biblical events took place in the land of Iraq. Abram the son of Terah (Gen 11:27) was called by God to leave everything behind him—including his country and his father's house—to go to the land that God himself would show him. Terah took his son Abram and his family and they left their city, Ur of the Chaldeans, to go into the land of Canaan. The ruins of this city are located in southern Iraq. Nineveh is another biblical city in Iraq, now known as Mosul. This city is located four hundred kilometers north of Baghdad, where I was born. Jonah was called by God to go to Nineveh, "that great city" (Jonah 1:2). It is now the second most populous city in Iraq after the capital, Baghdad. The remains of the old wall surrounding the city are still visible in places.

Iraq was one of the first places Christianity took root. According to church tradition, St. Thomas preached the gospel in Iraq while en route to India. Many churches and monasteries were built to glorify the Lord in Iraq, including the monastery of St. Matthew, which is located thirty-five

Global Christianity

kilometers northeast of the city of Nineveh. It was founded in the fourth century. Due to the persecution against Christians, St. Matthew the Hermit left his land in Turkey and established this monastery with other monks. We also know that there was a *Maferiono* (a Syriac ecclesiastical office) in Tikrit who held authority over bishops but remained under the authority of the Patriarch.

Christians in Iraq

Who are the Christians of Iraq? Christians in Iraq belong to the oldest local community of believers after Antioch. Early Christianity spread east of Antioch into Mesopotamia, present-day Iraq. Most of the Christians in Iraq still speak Aramaic, the language spoken by the Lord Jesus himself. Iraqi Christians belong to the following denominations: the Syrian Orthodox Church (which still uses Aramaic in their services and in homes), the Roman Catholic Church (which also uses Aramaic), the Church of the East (Assyrian), the Armenian Orthodox Church, the Coptic Orthodox Church, and a variety of Protestant churches.

Before the Gulf War in 1991, my experience was that Christians lived in relative peace and security. Granted, you were not free to speak out against the government, but radicals were prevented from attacking churches or kidnapping or killing Christians. Before 1991 Christians worshiped in their churches without fear of being persecuted. My people all remember how the church used to open for summer schools to educate children and youths ecclesiastically and biblically. Even after the Gulf War in 1991, during the embargo, which took so many years, the status quo continued; no one attacked churches or tried to kill Christians.

Everything changed with the American invasion in 2003.[1] The number of Christians in Iraq before 2003 was over one million. Most of them were living in Baghdad and Mosul in the north, which we call the Kurdish Area (Kurdistan), and in Basra, in the south. After the invasion, this number started to fall. The situation was complicated. Iraq was in chaos; society degenerated into a free-for-all. Christians were victims of this disordered situation. Islamic extremists started attacking Christians and their churches. Their hatred toward Christians grew. Christians were kidnapped, tortured, killed, and forcibly converted to Islam. Churches were

1. I left Iraq in 2001 to pastor a Syriac Orthodox church in Hamilton, Ontario, Canada.

bombed and women were ordered to wear the Islamic hijab in the streets, schools, and universities. Christians in Baghdad started leaving the city because militants were targeting them. Many churches were destroyed in Baghdad and Mosul.

The purpose of this ongoing persecution is to empty Iraq of Christians. It is not the first time Christians have endured persecution. The history of Christianity makes it clear that persecution is not something new; it has taken place since the beginning. Take, for instance, the genocide of over 1,000,000 Armenians in twentieth-century Turkey.[2] In addition to the Armenians, the Syriac Orthodox Church suffered, and thousands of its people who were living in south Turkey were killed or forced to leave the country. The people of Iraq were looking forward to a better life, including a democratic society, after the invasion. Unfortunately, the aftermath of the invasion left Iraq in a state opposite to their hopes and aspirations.

Muslim extremists harbor two accusations against Christians in Iraq. First, they call us "infidels" because we do not accept Islam. We must either convert to Islam or be killed. For them Christians are unbelievers. Any person who does not accept the Islamic faith is an infidel. Many Christians have been forced to convert to Islam. They would have been killed otherwise. Second, Christians are accused of being in league with the Americans. Since Americans are Christians, it follows that Iraqi Christians are allied with them. During the occupation, they accused Christians of cooperating with the Americans, especially when some Christians started working with the American army as translators. In retaliation, Muslim extremists "asked" for money from the church in order to fight the troops of the occupation.

The Persecution of My Family

My father was a priest in Mosul. He was forced to pay a ransom every month to religious extremists. These extremists claimed that they had the weapons and that Christians had the money needed to fight the American conquerors. They said, "It is either pay or be killed, so help us with the money and we will fight the conquerors. If the church does not cooperate, there will be consequences." My father was threatened many times. We still have the letters they used to send him. They used to put these letters under the door of the house so that he would see them when he woke up in the morning. Inside that envelope there was also a live bullet, which meant that

2. See chapter 7.

Global Christianity

they would kill him if he did not pay. They were watching him wherever he went. They used to call him on his phone and talk to him. Sometimes he did not answer their calls so they called the church. If the church said he was not there, they would claim to have just seen him entering the church. That was his first warning.

Our family received a threatening letter in early 2007. In October 2007 my youngest brother was killed outside of town. The situation in Iraq prevented those of us living outside of Iraq from attending the burial service. Immediately afterwards, my family received a second threatening letter. The man who came to the house was a Christian cooperating with the extremists. He tried to convince my father to give them money to support their mission of fighting the conquerors. My father's answer was, "Go and tell those who sent you to bring my son back." He then asked him to leave the house. The extremists continued to watch my father and to send threatening calls to his mobile and home phone. The family had to shut down all phones at home in order to avoid their threatening calls. This situation made it difficult for my father's family and friends to contact him. In the end, the church agreed to pay the money in order to save the lives of the congregation.

My sister and her husband received another threatening letter in April 2010. They tried to continue their lives, but at work he heard threats against "Crusaders" or "cousins of the Americans." The situation deteriorated, especially after the withdrawal of the US forces. The discrimination, persecution, and lack of security forced him to give up going to work. In fear and frustration they decided to leave the country because they did not see any other way forward. They left in October 2010.

The Persecution of Iraqi Christians

Not only were the clergy threatened, but also the laity. All Christians, especially those in prominent positions such as universities, business, and government, were in danger. Extremists forced female university students to wear the *hijab* (meaning they had to cover themselves from head to toe). They taunted Christians with epithets like "friends of Americans," "crusaders," and "infidels." We all remember the attack on 2 May 2010 on the road between Nineveh and the students' town "Bakhdeda."[3] One hundred and eighty-one

---

3. Sam Dagher, "Bombs Hit School Buses in North Iraq," *The New York Times*, 2 May 2010. Online: http://www.nytimes.com/2010/05/03/world/middleeast/03iraq.html

university students insisted that they would continue their studies because of their faith in Jesus. Their faith made them unafraid of death. Their only crime was to pursue an education in order to help rebuild their country.

Persecution in Iraq is not limited to students; clergy have also been targeted. In 2006, the Syriac Orthodox priest Boulos Iskander, the priest of St. Ephrem Syriac Church, was found decapitated on one of the streets in the city of Mosul.[4] He had been kidnapped a couple of days before. The kidnappers had asked for a ransom to free him, but while the church was negotiating with them, the kidnappers called the church saying, "We slaughtered him." Two years later, on 29 February 2008, the Chaldean Catholic Archbishop of Nineveh, Paulos Faraj Raho, was kidnapped while he was leaving the church of the Holy Spirit in the Al-Nur district. His kidnappers killed his two bodyguards and his driver. Raho succeeded in using his cell phone to call his church, asking them not to pay a ransom to free him. Among other things, his kidnappers were asking for three million dollars. He was tortured and killed. In March 2008 he was found dead in a grave near Mosul.[5]

Radical Muslims continue to persecute Christians. Any Christian who works in any company, office, or school is a potential target. It is a simple matter for them to confront and intimidate Christians. For instance, they might place a threatening note in the pocket of a Christian. They might start a conversation with them at work in the following manner, "Why do you not enter Islam? Why are you still living in darkness? Come to the illumination of Islam. Why do you not come and accept the true faith?" If a Christian refuses, they might put a sticker bomb under their car, which could explode any moment after they start driving. They declare publicly that no Muslim is allowed to buy a house from a Christian attempting to sell their house in order to leave the country. They say that one day they will acquire these houses without paying a single penny. In the future, they say, if a Christian family is forced leave their house or flees because of violence in their neighborhood, their house will be ceded to the Islamic state.

---

4. "Worldwide Christian Community Shocked as Priest Beheaded in Iraq," *Christianity Today*, October 17, 2006. Online: http://www.christiantoday.com/article/worldwide.christian.community.shocked.as.priest.is.beheaded.in.iraq/8023.htm (accessed June 2, 2014).

5. See Erica Goode, "Kidnapped Iraqi Archbishop is Dead," *The New York Times*, March 14, 2008. Online: http://www.nytimes.com/2008/03/14/world/middleeast/14iraq.html

Responding to Persecution

This situation has forced many Iraqi Christians to flee, just as I and many of my family have fled. They must either live in fear or flee. There is no other choice. At home they face expressions of hatred such as kidnapping, torture, and church bombings. Many churches in Baghdad and Mosul have been bombed. Muslim fanatics are sending Christians the clear message that they are not welcome in Iraq, and they must leave sooner or later.

Iraqi Christians in Baghdad and Mosul have begun to migrate to northern Iraq, hoping to find safety. But these migrants have found it difficult to find jobs and are unaccustomed to colder winters. Most of them have left the country for Syria or Jordan. Before the invasion, more than one million Christians lived in Baghdad, Nineveh, Basra, and in many towns and villages in the North. After the invasion, more than half of these left Iraq after becoming targets for Islamic extremists. The number of Christians in Iraq has dwindled to less than 300,000. Poor Christians unable to leave Iraq have moved to the North of Iraq along with those who do not want to leave their homeland. They are living there temporarily. If the situation continues like this, the remaining Christians will also leave for the havens of Europe, Australia, and North America. Right now there is no one to give them any assurance that they will be protected.

The church in Iraq is encouraging its faithful to stay. This has been our land for thousands of years; we are not strangers to this land. But what answer can the church provide to a family threatened with death by extremists? The church has often inspired the faithful to stay in their land, to stand firm in their faith against persecutions, and to be a witness for Christ. Most Christians in Iraq are unarmed. The church's message in Iraq is one of peace; this is the message of the Bible: peace and love and forgiveness according to the teaching of the Lord Jesus. As Christians, we have been called not to act violently but ethically, and seek to live in peace with our neighbors and with society. Jesus is not calling us to back out from this world but rather to go into the world and be witnesses for him as sheep in the midst of wolves. The martyrs in Iraq who offered themselves as living sacrifices believed that no one could separate them from the love of Jesus. They believed that carrying his cross is a way of dealing with problems in this world. As St. John says in his first letter, 5:19 "We know that we are God's children, and that the whole world lies under the power of the evil one." The church in Iraq is trying to do as much as it can to keep people from leaving the country. It offers help and support within its capacity, but the challenges that the Christians of

Iraq are facing are greater than those in the West can imagine. Thousands of them have fled to safer places where there is no killing, kidnapping, or oppression. Persecution in Iraq is not stopping; it has been increasing since 2003 and the faithful have had enough. They are looking for a better life for themselves and for their children in other lands that can offer them peace and safety.

Kenya: David Kirwa Tarus

I was born and brought up in a rural village in Uasin Gishu County in the former Rift Valley province of the fertile plateau of western Kenya. Uasin Gishu is the food basket of Kenya, being one of the leading producers of maize, wheat, dairy, and a variety of horticultural products. The headquarters of Uasin Gishu County is Eldoret, which is the home of world marathon and middle–distance runners. Eldoret is also a commercial city that attracts people from all over Kenya because of its cool and temperate climate, beautiful geographical features, highly arable land, educational institutions, and hospitals. Uasin Gishu is also home to several of Kenya's ethnic communities. The multi-ethnic dynamic of the County is one cause of its thriving economy. Christianity is the major religion in Uasin Gishu. The major denominations include the Africa Inland Church, the Anglican Church, and the Roman Catholic Church. My father is an evangelist serving with the Africa Inland Church.

I preached my first sermon when I was thirteen years old. My father had been invited as a guest preacher at a rural church ten kilometers from our home. We rode on a bicycle together. My father decided that he was going to train me to preach. So he asked me to preach. I was not prepared but I stood and delivered my first sermon, which went well according to various congratulatory messages I received after the service. My first sermon inspired me to consider full-time Christian ministry.

The simplicity of my story mirrors the simplicity of rural congregations in Kenya. It shows the fervor that rural evangelists have for developing a young generation of preachers. In rural Kenya the preacher might be anybody from a young teenager to an old man or woman. I was asked to teach Sunday school when I was barely in my teens. The need for trained leaders cannot be emphasized enough. According to *Operation World*, there are over 80,000 congregations in Kenya. Bible schools cannot train pastors and church workers fast enough. A pastor or an evangelist might be called upon to oversee up to five local churches. My father is a pastor of three churches that are about three kilometers apart. He does not have any formal theological training. Though he was a very brilliant student, earning himself the nickname *Makerere* (after the leading university in East Africa in the 60s and 70s), my father dropped out of primary school to take care of his ailing mother. My father's story is typical of many other pastors in rural churches in Kenya. Kenyan Christianity is marked by vibrant congregations, big numbers, and bicycling pastors. Rural pastors sometimes have to work in conditions of extreme poverty. It is a miracle that my parents have managed with so few resources to provide a university education for my siblings and myself.

The Urban Pastor

Whereas the rural pastor struggles with overseeing more than one congregation, the urban pastor struggles with the challenges of urban ministries. These may include multi-ethnicity, poverty, radical Islam, insecurity, and difficulties arising from the modernization of cities.

In terms of multi-ethnicity, most pastors serving in urban congregations came out of rural backgrounds and often lack experience in dealing with multi-ethnic congregations. Indeed, ethnicity is one of the major challenges in Kenya. Kenyan Christians have not been able to transcend ethnic divisions. The ethnic violence that followed the bungled 27 December 2007 general election was the worst in Kenya's history. Several churches were burnt down, at least one thousand people were killed, at least 500,000 people were internally displaced, and property worth billions of shillings was destroyed. The National Council of Churches of Kenya (NCCK) apologized to the people of Kenya for partisanship. The NCCK and other church agencies are trying to recover their voice in Kenya's socio-political landscape.

Perhaps the biggest challenge to urban churches in recent years is Islamic extremism and terrorism. Terrorist attacks on churches in Kenya since November 2011 have claimed many lives and injured hundreds of people. For example, on 1 July 2012 grenades were simultaneously hurled at worshippers in two churches in Garissa, a town in the northeastern region of Kenya. Our Lady of Consolata Catholic Church and the Africa Inland Church suffered casualties. The pastor of the Africa Inland Church, a man I have known since he was a student at the Missionary College in Eldoret, lost seventeen people including a close relative. These and many other attacks prompted a group of pastors in Mombasa in October 2013 to petition the government to issue them AK-47 rifles so that they could protect themselves and their congregations in case of an attack. The government is yet to act on this request. Urban pastors must find ways of doing ministry in the midst of such realities.

Church and Culture

In *Translating the Message*, Lamin Sanneh succinctly addresses the issue of the translation of the Christian faith. Translation means enabling others to appropriate the Christian faith in their local languages and idioms. The Church in Kenya is still grappling with how best to integrate the Christian faith with African culture and religion. Since the time missionaries brought the Christian faith to us, we have always attempted to find ways of practicing our faith without abandoning our culture. The dynamics associated with translating the gospel often lead to syncretism.

I remember growing up in a rural church that would lose almost half of the members during the season when the Kalenjin people circumcise their young boys (November to December) in the traditional coming-of-age ritual. Kalenjin Christians would abandon the church in order to successfully practice this, then reappear in January and ask for forgiveness. The cycle would be repeated again and again. Kalenjin Christians decided that the best way to address the challenge was to reevaluate the cultural practice by discarding those elements that were not compatible with biblical teaching and historic Christianity. The church therefore started a Christ-based circumcision movement whereby young boys were circumcised, taught the gospel, and prepared for adulthood. I belong to the third generation of this movement.

Although they have adopted some questionable theological positions, the African Independent or African Initiated Churches (AICs) have been successful in combining African culture and Christianity. The AICs cut links with missionary–founded churches. They were and are still more accommodating of African cultures. At times this leads to syncretism. Practices such as polygamy, female circumcision, and wife inheritance continue in some of these churches. In contrast, evangelicals and conservative denominations have largely abandoned these practices. Today, evangelical churches must engage African cultures, if they are to remain relevant.

Global Christianity

African Independent Churches are more appealing to the African peoples than evangelical and Protestant denominations for several reasons. First, AICs use African symbols, music, and instruments whereas many evangelical and Protestant denominations do not. AIC adherents are encouraged to express themselves through African dancing styles and rhythms. Second, their services are vibrant and charismatic. Third, they are very practically oriented churches; they practice their faith in very tangible ways. Their focus is the day-to-day lives of their people; they want to address the fear of the past, present, and future and the fear of spirits, death, life, and diseases. They promise to conquer, by the power of the Holy Spirit, all the binding powers of evil so that God's people are free to worship and to live lives of abundance. Fourth, they do not ignore spiritual warfare. AICs face spiritual forces head-on. Members are encouraged to lay all their fears before God; they are told that God is addressing their problems. They are promised victorious lives.

Taking spiritual conflict seriously resonates with the African worldview regarding spiritual beings (good and evil), and the constant opposition of bad spirits to whatever is good in the society. This emphasis explains the continued exponential growth of Pentecostal and charismatic movements in Kenya. It also explains why some mainstream Protestant churches in Kenya continue to embrace charismatic tendencies in their worship services. Philip Jenkins in *The Next Christendom* rightly observes that Christians of the global south "retain a very strong supernatural orientation."[6] Besides, Kenyan Christians are familiar with suffering, having experienced firsthand the HIV/AIDS pandemic that has led to the tragic death of thousands of people, oppressive regimes, corruption, ethnic conflicts, curable diseases that kill thousands of people, road carnage—at least 3,500 people die in road accidents in Kenya every year—and various environmental disasters. Kenyan Christians are looking for a faith that speaks to their quest for good health, spiritual and physical security, spiritual and material prosperity, a good afterlife, and a way to cope with all of the other ills and challenges mentioned above.

In contrast to the African Initiated Churches, evangelical and conservative churches (mainly the missionary instituted churches) tend to focus only on the mind. They stress things such as proper theology, in-depth Bible study, and Theological Education by Extension (TEE). Some marginalize matters of the heart, imagination, emotions, and the everyday concerns of

---

6. Jenkins, *Next Christendom*, 7.

the people. These churches are aloof from the social needs of the people and issues of spiritual warfare. It is therefore not uncommon that some members of evangelical churches attend their evangelical churches on a Sunday morning then an African Independent Church in the afternoon or during the week. There are also plenty of lunch-hour fellowships throughout the week to choose from.

The Church, the Bible, and Theology

God speaks my language! This particular exclamation points to the sheer joy of receiving a Bible in one's mother tongue. I feel immense satisfaction when I read a Kalenjin Bible. The message speaks to me in ways that an English Bible version cannot. However, there are still many ethnic communities that have not received the Bible in their language. In fact, there are at least twenty-two unreached people groups in Kenya.

Kenyan Christians have a very high view of the authority of Scripture. They appropriate the Bible in most cases without question. After a portion of Scripture is read in church, it is not uncommon to hear them exclaim things such as, "thank you Paul!" as if Paul himself was speaking to them. Philip Jenkins gets it right when he observes that Christians from the Global South rarely read Scripture abstractly, that Bible reading is intensely personal, and that the world of the Bible resonates with the world of Africa.[7] Indeed, we find in the Bible a message for everyday experiences. The Bible speaks to the challenge of poverty, environmental degradation, diseases, death, fear, polygamy, ethnocentrism, widowhood, single parenthood, injustice, corruption, and many other social and political issues. Kenyan Christians are generally morally and ethically conservative. It is expected that one take a stand against practices that are perceived to be unbiblical, such as abortion, homosexuality, and corruption.

The Kenyan church is aware that it needs to be self-propagating, self-governing, self-funding, and self-theologizing. The fourth "self" is indeed a mark of a maturing church. John Mbiti of Kenya lamented in 1969 the lack of a "theological consciousness and concern" in African churches.[8] This was true of the past, but times are changing. Kenyan Christians have now established their voice theologically. The Kenyan church has produced notable theologians such as John S. Mbiti, Jesse N. K. Mugambi, Samuel G. Kibicho,

7. Jenkins, *New Faces*.
8. Mbiti, "Some African Concepts," 51–52.

Nyambura J. Njoroge, Musimbi Kanyoro, Anne Nasimiyu Njoroge, Esther Mombo, James Kombo, and many others. In addition to academic theology, Kenya is replete with what Kwame Bediako calls "oral theology," the everyday theology of people as they seek to know God.[9] This theology can be deduced from sermons, Bible studies, Sunday school, songs, drama, stories, and so on. It plays the vital role of indicating how most Kenyan Christians think and talk about God, and how they envision themselves and their role in God's family.

Conclusion

I have provided a glimpse of the situation of the church in Kenya. The church is vibrant, robust, and growing in the midst of overwhelming challenges. It is my prayer that the church in Kenya will continue to grow, that pastors and evangelists serving in rural and urban churches will continue to serve even in difficult conditions, that Kenyan churches will discover the best way to integrate their culture into their worship without compromising their biblical faith, and that the church will provide a much-needed prophetic voice in Kenyan society.

SOUTH KOREA: SEONGHO KANG

When I was born, no one in my family believed in Jesus Christ. Confucianism was the dominant religion in my village and the religion practiced by my family. The moral rules of Confucianism forbid the people in my village from accepting Christianity as a religion. Christianity does not allow ancestor worship, which is one of the most important tenets of Confucianism. The widespread influence of Confucianism posed a significant obstacle to Christianity, not only for my family, but for others living in South Korea, especially in its rural areas. The cultural traditions of South Korea were clearly at work against the growth of Christianity.

Thankfully, a Christian teacher introduced me to Jesus in my second year of grade school. This was the first time I had heard about Jesus or the Christian religion. Even though I could not fully understand Christianity and was prohibited from attending a church by my parents, I felt a strong desire to learn about God.

---

9. Bediako, *Jesus and the Gospel*, 17.

While cultural traditions worked against the spreading of Christianity in South Korea, I noticed while growing up that Korean society appeared nonetheless to respect the church. Later I would learn that this was indeed the case. The reputation of Christianity had steadily improved from the time it was first introduced in Korea in the late 1800s. During my lifetime, however, this situation has changed. In my experience, the reputation of Christianity in Korea is on the decline.

The Korean Pentecost of 1907

Unlike other Protestant churches in Asian countries, the Protestant church in South Korea was properly established by Western missionaries within the past 120 years. The dominant religions of Confucianism and Buddhism acted as cultural barriers to the spread of Christianity. Back then, accepting Christianity often meant being ostracized by family and friends. Despite these challenges, however, Christianity gained a foothold in Korea.

The stature that Christianity would eventually enjoy in Korean society has its origins in immigration law. The prevailing authorities turned away the first missionaries to Korea and prohibited direct ministry to the Korean people. But they welcomed Westerners with skills in high demand. Therefore, the first missionaries into the country were also teachers and physicians. Since these first missionaries had many difficulties in direct evangelistic ministry, years of hard work yielded a disappointingly small number of converts. However, the Korean government had become dependent on the goodwill they generated and it was forced to ease restrictions on evangelism gradually in order to keep missionaries in the country.

Increased evangelism resulted in the Great Revival of 1907. Sometimes described as "the Korean Pentecost," the Great Revival of 1907 began during a Bible study meeting at a Presbyterian church in Pyongyang when hundreds of attendees felt overwhelmed by the Holy Spirit. The Great Revival ultimately resulted in an unprecedented spiritual experience for thousands of Christians across Korea and made a noticeable impact on their moral character. The movement has exercised a formative influence on the Korean church for a century.[10] According to Nak-chun Paek, who earned a PhD from Yale University and was the first church historian in Korea,

---

10. Yang, *Reformed Social Ethics*, 171–72.

> The most convincing argument for the genuineness of the revival is in the result that followed. The great awakening marks the spiritual rebirth of the Korean Church. The religious experience of the people gave to the Christian Church in Korea a character which is its own. Following the revival, the new religious experience was severely tested, but it has survived as a moral and spiritual force. Korean Christians of today look back on the movement as the source of their spiritual life.[11]

The revival also inaugurated several new characteristics of the Korean church, including: "early-morning prayer meetings, unison prayer in a loud voice, Bible studies, generous offerings, and zeal for evangelism."[12] The influence of this revival was seen everywhere in Korea. It rippled across the country and affected fledgling congregations from coast to coast.[13] Christians gathered to hold similar revivals where they recommitted themselves to living faithful lives. People who had joined the church "with various motives" now understood the meaning of "true repentance" and how they should live as Christians.[14] In addition, the Great Revival established new moral values in Korean Christians. After the revival, many Korean Christians proved their faith by making significant changes in their lifestyles.[15]

While the Great Revival triggered widespread spiritual excitement and a period of rapid growth for Christianity, it also disseminated the theological stance of the early missionaries, which was "conservative within the wide theological spectrum of nineteenth-century evangelicalism."[16] Since these missionaries were primarily interested only in spiritual spheres (and often had only a rudimentary understanding of Korean culture), the Korean church followed suit and limited its scope to spiritual spheres as well. As a result, Korean Christians drew a clear distinction between their spiritual lives and their secular, social, and political environments.

Even though the Great Revival inspired Korean Christians to repent of their sins, it did not motivate the Korean church to begin showing any special concern for socio-political issues.[17] Nevertheless, many individual

11. Paek, *Protestant Missions in Korea*, 374.
12. Lee, "Korean Pentecost," 81.
13. Ibid., 79.
14. Ibid., 73.
15. Ibid., 80.
16. Ryu, "Origin and Characteristics," 376–77.
17. Ibid., 393.

Christians attempted to practice their faith in the socio-political sphere, particularly when faced with the widespread brutalities of the Japanese colonial government that ruled Korea from 1910 to 1945.

The March First Movement in 1919 was the most significant civil protest up to that time against the Japanese colonial government. Many Korean people throughout the country gathered together and stood up for the independence of Korea. Ultimately, more than two million people participated in this demonstration and kept it going for more than a year. This movement was instrumental in drafting a formal *Declaration of Independence* that was presented to Japan. Christians played a vital role in the March First Movement. Even though the population of Christians in Korea was less than 5 percent at the time, "out of [the] 33 who signed the *Declaration of Independence*, 16 were Christians."[18]

The social stature of Christianity was already on the rise before this event. Christians were earning the admiration of their neighbors with their diligence, honesty, and generosity. The educational and medical services established by the first missionaries were badly needed. Christianity's stature climbed even faster after the March First Movement as Koreans took note of who was willing to stand against their oppressors.

Christianity remained highly-regarded in Korea for the next sixty years. But beginning in the 1990s, my opinion is that its stature began to slip, and in the same way the Great Revival accelerated its climb, a single event in 2007 exacerbated its slide.

The Afghan Hostage Crisis of 2007

In 2007, on the 100th anniversary of the Great Revival, Korean Protestant church leaders asked Koreans to pray for another revival. However, while we prayed for a revival, God gave us two martyrs. The incident is known in Korea as the Afghan Hostage Crisis of 2007. It began when members of the Taliban captured twenty-three Korean Christian volunteers working in Afghanistan and held them hostage. Two of the hostages were killed, whereas the others were released two months later.

The volunteers were sent to Afghanistan by Sammul Church, which was built in 1998 by Seoul Youngdong Church in Korea. One of the hostages killed by the Taliban was the pastor of my home church, Seoul Youngdong Church, where he had preached for many years.

18. Yang, *Reformed Social Ethics*, 179.

I remember how the incident captured the attention of South Korea for the two months the captives were held hostage. Both Christians and the larger public called on the Korean government to intervene and attempt to save the lives of the captives. But some people directed hostile rhetoric toward Christianity and Sammul Church in particular. Protestors argued that Korean Christians were evangelizing too aggressively in Islamic nations. They also claimed that the church and its volunteers ignored warnings from the Korean government about performing relief work in Afghanistan.

This incident not only affected Christians, but also the international relationships of the South Korean government with other countries such as the USA and Afghanistan. "The South Korean government's decision to negotiate directly with the Taliban" faced "muted criticism from Afghan and U.S. officials."[19] In this context, the South Korean public expressed their anger towards the hostages and the Korean Protestant church. Due to this public anger, the Korean hostages should have apologized for their mission travel at a press center.[20] Yu Kyeong-sik, one of hostages, said, "I've had sleepless nights, thinking of what we have caused the country. I am deeply sorry."[21]

Most of the hostages were medical professionals doing medical work. Since I know many of them personally, I can say that they were not aggressively evangelizing Afghans. Even though I could raise many points in defense of the relief workers, my point is not to defend them or Sammul Church, it is to point out the widespread hostility they faced from the majority of Koreans. This incident clearly shows how radically Korean perception of Christianity has changed from what it was at the time of the Great Revival.

The Reason for the Reversal

Even though the Korean church accomplished amazing growth within a period of one hundred years, it is now experiencing a reversal. The number of Protestant Christians in Korea has decreased over the past couple of decades.[22] The Korean public shows increasing hostility toward the Korean Protestant church. One hundred years ago, the Korean Protestant church was complimented by non-Christians and welcomed by Korean society. The reverse is true today.

19. Bailey, "In the Aftermath," 65.
20. Ibid.
21. Ibid.
22. Hong, "Korean Protestantism," 216–17.

From the early 1950s to the late 1980s, South Korea was ruled by authoritarian governments. For most of that period, South Korea was under a military dictatorship. During this time, the Korean evangelical conservative Protestant church concentrated on growing its membership rather than showing compassion for the immense suffering occurring in the public square.[23]

Today the public does not trust the Korean Protestant church. According to most Korean Christian ethics scholars and the Christian Ethics Movement of Korea (a Christian public policy institution), an unfortunate side effect of the evangelical movement in Korea is increased competition. Churches in South Korea number in the tens of thousands—all within a country about the size of the state of Indiana. Churches compete so intensely for members that pastors are compelled to take extreme positions to stand out from the others. As a result of this competition, pastors often do not emphasize moral behavior that is consistent with the Christian faith. In other words, pastors lose sight of the good deeds that are supposed to accompany faith (Jas 2:13–26). The Korean Protestant church has not taught proper Christian morality to Korean society and the Korean public has taken notice.[24]

According to Sebastian Kim, an editor of *International Journal of Public Theology*, it is obvious that the Korean Protestant church has lost the credibility and respect of the Korean people. He argues that "the contemporary Protestant church is facing a crisis in public life" based on a recent survey that "demonstrates a 'credit crunch' for the Korean Protestant Churches in the form of a serious problem of credibility among the general public."[25] When the Christian Ethics Movement of Korea analyzed the popular social credibility of the Protestant church, it found that only 18 percent of Koreans view Christians as trustworthy and credible. This low score is correlated to the immorality of Christians in Korean society. Both Christians and non-Christians in Korean society are highly critical of the behavior of Christians in Korea. The Korean Protestant church is expected to demonstrate behavior that is consistent with their faith.

---

23. Son and Raj, "Socio-Political Issues," 15.
24. Hong, "Korean Protestantism," 220.
25. Kim, "Editorial," 133.

Conclusion

Public regard for Christianity and the Korean Protestant church has changed radically since the first missionaries reached Korea in the late-1800s. One hundred years ago, Korean people found it difficult to accept Christianity because it conflicted with certain moral rules of Confucianism and established cultural traditions. Nevertheless, Christians earned the respect of Koreans by contributing to the independence of Korea and living out Christian values.

Korean Protestant Christians still have a strong desire for evangelical work and missions. This desire contributed to the amazing growth of the Korean Protestant church over one hundred years. Many of them still work towards the common good of our society, but it cannot be denied that Korean public opinion has changed to the point where a majority of non-Christians feel disgust or hostility toward the Christian church. The Korean Protestant church was lauded one hundred years ago for its benevolence toward others and our country; now it is criticized for its indifference to the suffering of others and its apathy towards the common good. The Korean Protestant church cannot avoid the expectations of Korean society. The Afghan Hostage Crisis served to highlight its declining social credibility, making it clear that the church must change its ways in order to thrive once more. The Korean Protestant church can contribute to the common good of Korean society and once again earn the respect of the Korean people if it acts in a way that is consistent with the faith it professes. It needs to show civility and compassion to others in the public square.

Bibliography

Bailey, Sarah Pulliam. "In the Aftermath of a Kidnapping: The South Korean Missionary Movement Seeks to Mature without Losing Its Zeal." *Christianity Today* 51, no. 11, 1 November 2007, 64–65.

Bediako, Kwame. *Jesus and the Gospel in Africa: History and Experience*. Maryknoll, NY: Orbis, 2004.

Hong, Young-Gi. "Korean Protestantism to the Present Day." In *The Blackwell Companion to Protestantism*, edited by Alister E. McGrath, 216–21. Malden: Blackwell, 2004.

Jenkins, Philip. *The New Faces of Christianity: Believing the Bible in the Global South*. Oxford: Oxford University Press, 2006.

———. *The Next Christendom: The Coming of Global Christianity*. Oxford: Oxford University Press, 2002.

Kim, Sebastian C. H. "Editorial: [the Idea of the 'Public Sphere']." *International Journal of Public Theology* 6, no. 2 (January 1, 2012) 131–35.

Lee, Young Hoon. "Korean Pentecost: The Great Revival of 1907." *Asian Journal of Pentecostal Studies* 4, no. 1 (January 1, 2001) 73–83.

Mbiti, John. "Some African Concepts of Christology." In *Christ and the Younger Churches: Theological Contributions from Asia, Africa and Latin America*, edited by Georg F. Vicedom, 51–62. London: SPCK, 1972.

Paek, Nak-chun. *The History of Protestant Missions in Korea, 1832–1910*. 2nd ed. Seoul: Yonsei University Press, 1971.

Ryu, Dae-Young. "The Origin and Characteristics of Evangelical Protestantism in Korea at the Turn of the Twentieth Century." *Church History* 77, no. 2 (June 1, 2008) 371–98.

Sanneh, Lamin. *Translating the Message: The Missionary Impact on Culture*. Rev. ed. Maryknoll, NY: Orbis, 2009.

Son, Bong-Ho, and Ebenezer Sunder Raj. "Can the Evangelist Ignore Socio-Political Issues?" *Transformation* 8 (January 1, 1991) 15–19.

Yang, Nak Heong. *Reformed Social Ethics and the Korean Church*. New York: P. Lang, 1997.

Author Index

Abella, Irving, 106, 107, 123
Adeney, Francis S., 42, 50
Adiwardana, Margaretha, 137, 138
Akcam, Taner, 111, 120, 124
Allen, John L., Jr., 22, 24, 30
Althouse, Peter, 12, 85, 87, 104
Angus, Murray E., 116, 117, 124
Aquinas, Thomas, 101, 103
Arissian, Nora, 106, 124
Arnott, John, 93, 94, 96, 103
Arpin-Ricci, Jamie, 39, 50
Augustine, 56, 57
Auron, Tair, 122, 124
Avotri, Solomon, 79, 84

Bacote, Vincent E., 59, 68
Bailey, Sarah Pulliam, 155, 158
Balakian, Peter, 106, 124
Bardakjian, Kevork, 106, 124
Barton, James L., 109, 124
Beach, Lee, 11, 31, 36, 51, 53
Bediako, Kwame, 151, 158
Berger, Carl, 116, 124
Bessenecker, Scott, 39, 50
Bevans, Stephen B., 98, 103
Beyerhaus, Peter P. J., 131, 134, 138
Bibby, Reginald Wayne, 31, 33, 34, 50
Black, Binney S., 120
Bloxham, Donald, 106, 118, 122, 124
Bolger, Ryan K., 41, 44, 50, 52, 68
Bosch, David J., 97, 98, 103, 137, 138
Bowler, Kate, 107, 124
Boyd-MacMillan, Ronald, 129, 138
Brewer, Charles G., 117, 124

Broadhead, Bradley K., 1
Brown, J. G., 118, 119
Buckner, Philip, 116, 124
Bullinger, Heinrich, 74
Burns, Scott, 54, 68

Campbell, Heidi, 38, 50
Carson, D. A., 46, 50, 55
Cavanaugh, William T., 3, 13
Chambers, L. P., 114, 115, 119
Charmaz, Kathy, 103
Chu, Jeff, 56, 68
Claiborne, Shane, 39, 50, 54
Cole, Douglas, 116, 124
Collins, Randall, 95, 103
Cook, Terry, 116, 124
Cullmann, Oscar, 131

Dadrian, Vahakn N., 105, 106, 111, 124
Dagher, Sam, 143
Dau, Isaiah Majok, 138
Davidson, Melissa, 46, 117, 124
Davis, Leslie A. , 106, 109, 124
Davison, Andrew, 50
Dekmejian, R. Hrair, 106, 125
Demarest, Bruce A., 58, 59, 68
Derderian, Katherine, 112, 125
Dobkin, Marjorie Housepian, 106, 125
Duin, Julia, 34, 50
Dunn, James D. G., 63, 68
Dyrness, William A., 129, 138

Endicott, James, 119, 120
Engel, James F., 129, 138

Author Index

Erichsen, Casper W., 105, 127
Erickson, Millard J., 58, 59, 68
Estes, Doug, 38, 50

Felcher, Marilyn, 127
Ferguson, Niall, 110, 125
Fernando, Ajith, 136, 138
Fletcher, Richard, 3, 13
Fowler, Michelle, 117, 125
Frost, Michael, 41, 50

Genizi, Haim, 125
Gibbs, Eddie, 41, 44, 50
Glaser, Barney G., 91, 103
Goldman, Francisco, 28, 30
Goode, Erica, 144
Gorman, Michael, 82, 84
Graber, G. S., 105, 112, 122, 125
Green, John C., 91, 104
Greidanus, Sidney, 74, 84
Grim, Brian J., 138
Grudem, Wayne A., 59, 68
Grundmann, Walter, 79, 84
Guant, David, 106, 112, 125
Guder, Darrell L., 100, 103
Guroian, Vigen, 109, 125

Hanciles, Jehu J., 2, 3, 4, 5, 13,
Hartenstein, Karl, 138
Hartshorne, Charles, 101, 103
Hastings, Adrian, 5, 13
Hauerwas, Stanley, 54
Heath, Gordon L., 12, 105, 106, 116, 125, 135, 138
Henderson, Jim, 43, 50
Hiebert, Paul G., 7, 13
Higgins, John R., 59, 68
Hofmann, Tessa, 112, 125
Hong, Young-Gi, 155, 158
Hood, Ralph, Jr., 88
Hopkins, J. Castell, 110, 125
Horton, Stanley M., 59, 68
Hovannisian, Richard G., 106, 109, 111, 126, 127, 128
Howell, Richard, 130, 139
Hunsberger, George R., 100, 103
Hunter, Todd, 43, 50

Hybels, Bill, 55
Hylson-Smith, Kenneth, 1, 5, 9, 13

Isaak, John Haitham, 12, 10, 140

Jenkins, Philip, 1, 6, 7, 8, 10, 13, 15, 22, 30, 31, 49, 50, 69, 70, 71, 84, 109, 126, 149, 150, 158
Johnson, Rolf M., 92, 103

Kaiser, Hilmar, 118, 126
Kalu, Ogbu U., 2, 13
Kang, Seongho, 10, 12, 13, 140, 151, 158
Kanyoro, Musimbi, 27, 30, 151
Khosroeva, Anahit, 112, 126
Kibicho, Samuel G., 150
Kiernan, Ben, 105, 126
Kim, Sebastian C. H., 156, 158
Kirakossian, Arman J., 106, 126
Kitamori, Kazoh, 101, 103
Kloian, Richard, 106, 126
Knowles, Michael P., 10, 69, 74, 84
Kombo, James, 151
Kotlikoff, Laurence, 54, 68
Kuper, Leo, 106, 107, 111, 126
Kuyper, Abraham, 59, 68

Law, Stephen, 5, 13
Lee, Matthew T., 88, 89, 103, 132, 134
Lee, Young Hoon, 153, 158
Lee, Young Kee, 139
Lemkin, Raphael, 108
Lewis, C. S., 6, 13
Lewy, Guenter, 126
Lifton, Robert Jay, 128
Long, Thomas G., 75, 84
Luther, Martin, 74, 131, 139

Macchia, Frank, 101, 104
MacDonald, Stuart, 117, 126
MacMillan, Margaret, 122, 126
Marashlian, Levon, 112, 127
Markusen, Eric, 128
Marshall, David B., 31, 51
Marshall, Paul A., 129, 139
Martin, Lawrence T., 84
Masenya, Madipoane, 28, 30

Author Index

Mbiti, John S., 150, 158
McCauley, Leo P., 79, 84
McConnell, Douglas, 9, 13
McFague, Sallie, 60, 68
McKnight, Scot, 45, 46, 51
McLaren, Brian, 43, 51
Meconi, David Vincent, 73, 84
Melson, Robert, 111, 127
Menzies, William W., 59, 68
Milbank, Alison, 46, 50
Miller, Donald E., 109, 116, 127
Moltmann, Jürgen, 101, 104
Mombo, Esther, 151
Moo, Douglas J., 63, 68
Moranian, Suzanne E., 106, 127
Morganthaler, Sally, 40, 51
Morton, A. S., 120
Mugambi, Jesse N. K., 150
Murray, J. Lovell, 119
Murray, Stuart, 2, 8, 13

Nassibian, Akaby, 106, 127
Nefsky, Alan Davies, 107, 127
Netland, Harold A., 6, 7, 13
Newbigin, Lesslie, 71, 78, 84, 100, 104
Nichanian, Marc, 109, 127
Njoroge, Anne Nasimiyu, 151
Njoroge, Nyambura J., 151
Noll, Mark A., 22, 30
Nystrom, Carolyn, 22, 30

Oke, Mim Kemal, 109, 127
Olusoga, David, 105, 127
Ostergaard, Karen, 127

Paek, Nak-chun, 152, 153, 158
Page, Robert, 116, 127
Pagitt, Doug, 45
Payaslian, Simon, 106, 127
Penlington, Norman, 116, 128
Penner, Glenn, 132, 139
Peroomian, Rubina, 109, 128
Peters, Ted, 101, 104
Peterson, Eugene H., 84
Peterson, Merrill D., 106, 128
Pinnock, Clark, 94, 98, 99, 104
Piper, John, 55

Pobee, John S., 24, 30
Pocock, Michael, 9, 13
Poloma, Margaret M., 88–91, 103, 104
Porter, Andrew, 4, 14
Porter, Stanley E., 138
Post, Stephen G., 88, 89, 103
Purchas, Samuel, 15, 30
Purves, Andrew, 75, 84

Raj, Ebenezer Sunder, 156, 158
Ramachandra, Vinoth, 78, 79, 84
Ranns, H. D., 120
Reimer, Reg, 138, 139
Rexford, Principal, 120
Richards, Samuel J., 116, 117, 128
Ricoeur, Paul, 75, 84
Ryu, Dae-Young, 153, 158

Sanneh, Lamin O., 5, 14, 22, 30, 79, 84, 148, 158
Sarafian, Ara, 109, 128
Sarkissian, S. H., 114
Sauer, Christof, 11, 129, 130, 133, 138, 139
Schirrmacher, Thomas, 138, 139
Schroeder, Roger P., 98, 103
Schweitzer, Albert, 88
Semple, Neil, 107, 128
Shantz, Mary-Ann, 107, 128
Shirinian, Lorne, 106, 109, 113, 128
Silver, A. I., 116, 128
Smith, Roger W., 109, 128
Smoakian, Manoug Joseph, 111, 122, 128
Son, Bong-Ho, 156, 158
Sookhdeo, Patrick, 138, 139
Sorokin, Pitirim, 12, 88, 89, 104
Spinks, Craig, 43, 50
Stanley, Brian, 4, 9, 14
Stephenson, Anthony A., 79, 84
Sterk, Vernon Jay, 139
Stone, Bryan, 51
Straus, Anselm L., 91, 103
Studd, C. T., 59
Studebaker, Steven M., 1, 11, 36, 51, 52

Tarus, David Kirwa, 10, 12, 13, 140, 146
Taylor, Charles, 31, 51

Author Index

Taylor, William D., 138, 139
Temple, William, 5
Ternon, Yves , 109, 128
Theriault, Henry C., 109, 128
Thomlinson, Dave, 43, 51
Tiénou, Tite, 7, 14
Tiessen, Terrance L., 58, 68
Tieszen, Charles, 130, 139
Ton, Josef, 133, 137, 139
Touryan, Lorna, 109, 127
Troper, Harold, 106, 107, 123

van der Meer, Antonia Leonora, 139
Van der Meer, Tonica, 138, 139
Van Gelder, Craig, 100, 103, 104
Van Rheenen, Gail, 9, 13
Vanhoozer, Kevin J., 8, 14
Versteeg, Peter, 100, 102, 104
Videlier, Philippe, 106, 128

Walker, C. J., 106, 118, 128
Wallis, Jim, 23
Walls, Andrew, 2, 3, 14
Warren, Rick, 55
Weitbrecht, H. U., 120
Weitz, Eric D., 108, 128
Wespetal, Thomas J. , 138, 139
Westfall, Cynthia , 138
Wilkinson, Michael, 12, 85, 87, 104
Williams, David, 117
Winter, Jay, 106, 128
Wright, William J., 56, 68

Yang, Nak Heong, 152, 154, 158
Yildirim, Onur, 123, 128
Yoder, John Howard, 54
Yong, Amos, 103

Zdero, Rad, 37, 51

Subject Index

1.5 generation, 71–72

Afghan Hostage Crisis of 2007, 154–155, 157
Africa, 9, 17, 22, 24, 69
Africa Inland Church, 146
African Independent or Initiated Churches, 148
African Kingdom of Congo, 4
Anabaptists, 3
Anglican Church, 146
appreciative-love, 92
Armenian Christianity, 114
Asia, 17, 20, 22, 69
Assemblies of God, 91
Augustine, 56–57

Babel, 75–78
Bad Urach Statement, 130, 137
Bible, Scripture, 4, 5, 8
Britain, 19
British Empire, 4
Buddhism, 26, 152

care-love, 92
Catch the Fire, 86–88
Cathars, 3
catholic, 25
charismatic (faith), 22–23, 25
Christian Ethics Movement of Korea, 156
chronological snobbery, 6
citizen sojourners, 61–67
classical theism, 101
club Christianity, 55–56
colonialism, 5, 7

common grace, 58–59
Confucianism, 26, 151, 152
consumerism, 65
creation, 60–61
cross-cultural testimony, 80
crucifixion, 74, 75
cruciform, 82

demonology, 24
discipleship, 41, 132

East India Company, 4
emerging church, 35
empire, 63
English as a Second Language (ESL), 9
eschatological hope, 101
eschatology, 136
Europe, 1, 15, 17, 18, 19, 21
evangelical, 25
evangelism, 41–42
exorcism, 24

First World War, 105
fortress Christianity, 55

Genocide Convention, 108
genocide, 108–109
global church, 7
Global North, 22
Global South, 4, 7, 8, 9, 17, 18, 25
gospel, 9
Great Commandment, 95, 100
Great Commission, 95, 99, 100
Gulf War, 141

Hamidian Massacres, 110–111

163

Subject Index

healing, 24
Holy Spirit, 82
house churches, 36–37
Humpty Dumpty theology, 53, 56–59

imago Dei, 98
incarnational, 42
internet church, 37–38
Iraqi Christians, 140–146
irony of preaching, 83
Islam, 20–21, 26–27, 144

Jesus, 44–45, 132, 133
Jewish Holocaust, 106, 109, 121
John, the Apostle, 62, 65–66

Kalenjin Christians, 148
Kenyan Christians, 146–151
Kingdom theology, 39
Korean Christians, 151–157
Korean Pentecost, 152

Latin America, 17, 22, 52
liturgical, 25

March First Movement, 154
margins Christianity, 54
martyrdom, 135–136
message of the cross, 73
method of cross-cultural preaching, 81–83
missio dei, 82, 97–98
missiology, 129
mission, 98–99
missional, 42, 45, 48
missionaries, 3, 4, 6
monastery of St Matthew, 140

National Council of Churches of Kenya, 147
new monastics, 38–39
North America, 17, 18, 21

Old Testament, 28–29
Operation World, 146
Ottoman Empire, 105, 110. 111, 118

Paul, the Apostle, 62–65
Peace of Westphalia, 3

Pentecost, 78–80
persecution, 134, 145–146
Peter, the Apostle, 73–74, 79
Portuguese Catholics, 4
post-Christendom, 6, 8, 52–53
post-Christian culture, 45
post-colonial thought, 7
postmodern culture, 45
prayer, 98
process theology, 101

reconciliation, 83
redemption, 60–61
religious affiliation, 32–33
religious extremists, 142–143
resurrection, 75
reward, 137
Roman Catholic Church, 24–25, 146
Roman Empire, 2

Second World War, 2, 7, 106–107, 121
signs and wonders, 96–97
soaking prayer, 86, 89, 92
social gospel, 47–48
social justice, 42
South America, 69
special grace, 58–59
spiritual warfare, 23
suffering, 131–134
syncretism, 148
Syriac Orthodox Church, 142

Taoism, 26
Thirty-Years War (Wars of Religion), 3, 3n11
Toronto Airport Christian Fellowship, 86
Toronto blessing, 85, 89
translation, 148
Treaty of Lausanne, 122
trinitarian theology, 101

union-love, 92
United Kingdom, 9

Western Christianity, 1, 5–6, 7, 15
Western theology, 7, 8, 130
worship, 40–41

Young Turks, 111

Scripture Index

OLD TESTAMENT

Gen 3:15	66	Ruth	71
Gen 11	76		
Gen 11:1–9	75	Neh 9:26	131
Gen 11:6–8	76		
Gen 11:27	140	Job 31:32	9
Lev 26:14-39	131	Jer 29:8	62
Deut 7	136	Jonah 1:2	140

NEW TESTAMENT

Matt 2:13–14	131	Luke 1:49	79
Matt 5:45	136	Luke 4:14–30	131
Matt 6:10	60	Luke 9:23	131
Matt 10:17	133	Luke 9:43	79
Matt 16:22	73	Luke 10:27	87
Matt 22:37, 39	87	Luke 12:15	65
Matt 23:37	131	Luke 14:28–30	77
Matt 24:13	133	Luke 14:33	77
Matt 24:9–14	135	Luke 22:28–30	137
Matt 24:9–25	136	Luke 24:46–49	77
Matt 25:35	9		
		John 1:4	135
Mark 10:32	74	John 1:11	135
Mark 12:30–31	87	John 1:12–13	82
Mark 14:27–31	74	John 12:24	133
Mark 14:50	74	John 12:24	135

Scripture Index

John 12:26	133	2 Cor 4:7–10	135
John 12:32	133	2 Cor 4:17	137
John 15:18–16:4	65	2 Cor 12:9–10	135, 136
John 15:20a	133		
John 17:18	131	Gal 3:28	80
John 18:37	131		
John 20:19, 21	77	Eph 2:13–14	81
John 20:21	131	Eph 2:17–18	81
John 21:18–19	136	Eph 3:8	81
		Eph 3:12	81
Acts 2:4	78	Eph 3:17–20	93
Acts 2:6–8	78		
Acts 2:11	78	Phil 1:12–16	134
Acts 2:16–18	79	Phil 1:20	136
Acts 2:21	80	Phil 2:6–11	137
Acts 2:39	80	Phil 2:12	59
Acts 4:2–30	137		
Acts 5:18	133	Col 1:24	134
Acts 7:55	137		
Acts 8:1–3	74	1 Thess 2	136
Acts 8:14–17	80		
Acts 10:44–46	80	2 Tim 2:10	134
Acts 12:2	133	2 Tim 2:12	137
Acts 20:24	136	2 Tim 3:1–13	136
Rom 8:17	137	Heb 2:9	137
Rom 8:17–18	137	Heb 2:14–18	131
Rom 8:19–22	136	Heb 2:18	133
Rom 8:20–21	60	Heb 5:8	131
Rom 8:31–39	133	Heb 11:14–15	76
Rom 12:1	136	Heb 13:2	9
Rom 14:8	136		
Rom 15:7	9	James	71
		James 2:13–26	156
1 Cor 1:18	73, 135, 136		
1 Cor 1:21–23	73	1 Pet 1:11	137
1 Cor 1:23	135	1 Pet 2:12	137
1 Cor 1:31	136	1 Pet 2:21–24	131
1 Cor 2:1	73	1 Pet 4:13–14	137
1 Cor 2:3–5	82	1 Pet 4:14	137
1 Cor 4:20	82	1 Pet 5:9	134
1 Cor 12:26	134		
1 Cor 15:1	73	2 Pet 3:4	136
1 Cor 15:58	136	2 Pet 3:9	136
2 Cor 1:3–11	133	1 John 2:18	136
2 Cor 4:5	75	1 John 3:8	133

Scripture Index

1 John 5:19	145	Rev 21:1–5	136
		Rev 21:3–4	66
Revelation	71	Rev 21:7–8	133
Rev 1:5	131	Rev 22	61
Rev 13–19	136	Rev 22:20	66
Rev 15:2–4	137	Rev 3:12	137
Rev 16:5–6	136	Rev 3:14	131
Rev 17:6	136	Rev 3:21	137
Rev 19:2	137	Rev 6:9–11	136
Rev 19:6–10	136	Rev 6:11	134
Rev 20:4	137	Rev 7:9–17	137

www.ingramcontent.com/pod-product-compliance
Lightning Source LLC
Chambersburg PA
CBHW071458150426
43191CB00008B/1381